"*Alexa Joy Sherman and Nicole Tocantins have done for sexuality in the 21st century what Helen Gurley Brown's* Sex and the Single Girl, *Erica Jong's* Fear of Flying, *and Cynthia Heimel's* Sex Tips for Girls *did for it in the 20th. If you're a single woman seeking sexual liberation or simply a guy looking for insight into the female mind, this oft-hilarious book offers equal parts solid factual advice and anecdotal evidence.*"

—ROY TRAKIN, senior editor at *HITS Magazine*

"*A hot, random act of carnalness is one of life's must-dos. If you want to know the secrets of pulling off a successful one-night stand (sans guilt, stalkers, heartbreak, and itchy rashes), this book is not afraid to tell it like it is. These women clearly know what they're talking about.*"

—COLLEEN RUSH, author of *Swim Naked, Defy Gravity & 99 Other Essential Things to Accomplish Before Turning 30*

"*Nicole and Alexa Joy have combined the perfect mix of humor, intellect, and insig*_____*lly entertaining and enlighte*_____*s! Men everywhere would b*_____*st, funny, and compelling b*_____*"

—DAVID ADELSON, producer/_____ at E! Entertainment Television

*"Ditching the guilt and double standards that exist for horny women, Alexa and Nicole combine colorful firsthand tales of hook-ups with a no-nonsense approach to finding and getting sex, empowering women to take control of their own pleasure."*

—ANNA SKINNER, author of *How to Pee Standing Up: Tips for Hip Chicks*

*"Finally, a take-no-prisoners (unless they're cute) guide to female sexuality in a post-feminist era. I loved this book, and so will anyone who likes to read—and loves sex!"*

—DAN BUCATINSKY, actor/writer/producer at Is or Isn't Entertainment

# The
# Happy Hook-Up

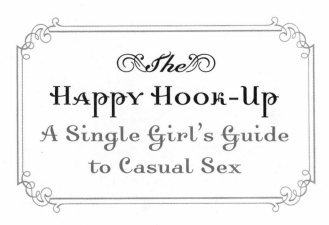

# The
# Happy Hook-Up
# A Single Girl's Guide
# to Casual Sex

Alexa Joy Sherman
and Nicole Tocantins

TEN SPEED PRESS
Berkeley | Toronto

Ten Speed Press
Box 7123
Berkeley, California 94707
www.tenspeed.com

Distributed in Australia by Simon and Schuster Australia,
in Canada by Ten Speed Press Canada, in New Zealand by
Southern Publishers Group, in South Africa by Real Books, and
in the United Kingdom and Europe by Airlift Book Company.

Design by Catherine Jacobes Design, San Francisco

Library of Congress Cataloging-in-Publication Data

Sherman, Alexa Joy.
The happy hook-up : a single girl's guide to casual sex / Alexa
Joy Sherman and Nicole Tocantins.
    p. cm.
 Includes index.
 ISBN 1-58008-609-8 (pbk.)
1.  Women--Sexual behavior.  I. Tocantins, Nicole. II. Title.
 HQ29.S534 2004
 306.7'082--dc22

                              2004017628

Printed in Canada
First printing, 2004

1 2 3 4 5 6 7 8 9 10 — 08 07 06 05 04

# ◌Contents◌

*You're So Good!*

(ACKNOWLEDGMENTS)

Please indulge us for a moment or two as we give big ups to everyone who made this book possible—for without these people, we may not have written it (so feel free to blame them).

Above all, Alexa thanks Joel for his unwavering support—on this project, in life, in love—and Nicole, for the friendship and the concept, for bringing the funny and seeing it through. Nicole thanks Alexa for believing wholeheartedly in the idea for this book and being there as writing partner and friend. Alexa and Nicole both thank their amazing friends for their unrelenting support, inspiration, and laughter (you shall all remain nameless, given the fact that your stories are in here). Oh—and we thank Ruby and Sydney, too.

We thank our families—especially our parents, who were able to finally find love after what we imagine were many wonderful casual sex encounters (at least a few? one?). Thanks to Alexa's parents for being so vocal about sexuality, from the gifts of *Where Did I Come From?* and *What's Happening to Me?* to the too-much-information-at-the-dinner-table discussions—and to Nicole's parents for being so reserved that Nicole had to go out and get some pronto.

Of course, to the men who came before the current ones (in more ways than one), who screwed us literally and figuratively: Thank you for what you were able to offer, meager as it may have been. Hey, we got a book out of it, didn't we? To the guys who treated us like goddesses and took us for the rides of our lives: we are far more indebted to you than you'll ever know—for you made us realize that sex can seriously rock, and we deserve to get off as much as you (if not more). Thanks, guys.

Many thanks to Stacey Glick, who had faith in the fact that this book was worth publishing—that no matter how many women out there already know how to have sex for sport, they could still use a tip or two (as could the women who don't know how to do it and who just might want a little enlightenment on the matter). We must also thank the friends and mentors who offered guidance and support along the way—especially Eric Harr, for an incredibly happy hook-up (you know what we mean)—and everyone at Ten Speed Press, particularly our editor Julie Bennett: Thank you for believing in two girls and their perverse dream.

We send our deepest gratitude to all of the experts who weighed in with advice, as well as to all the people out there, friends and otherwise, who filled out questionnaires, wrote in with their stories and suggestions, and generally just put out and kept on putting out. In a nutshell, thank you.

*Preface*

Casual sex. Who knew it could be so complicated? After all, the word "casual" carries with it an implication of carelessness and simplicity—but perhaps that's where the problems begin. As much as no-strings-attached action may be a spur-of-the-moment experience, we've come to realize that being careless can make casual sex a lot less fun for a girl, both physically and emotionally. That's why we urge you to think through it as completely as possible. We understand that comprehensive consideration of the details can prove elusive when you go out to a bar, get completely trashed, meet a really hot guy, and decide all you want to do is him. This is one of the many reasons we wrote this book.

In the interest of full disclosure, though, while we've certainly done hard time in the casual sex trenches, please understand we are in no way trained professionals (though some guys we've encountered have told us we should be—hey, was that a compliment, or . . . ?). We share our own—and other women's—stories and advice in an effort to make the situations in which you may find yourself more empowering, enjoyable, safe, and sane. And while we complement all of this with information and tips from a variety of reputable sources and select experts (as well as a few people of the male persuasion), we cannot take responsibility for any harm, physical or otherwise, that may result from following the advice herein, nor can the experts or publisher.

Also, in the event that you're wondering where the hell we came up with some of the information in this book:

- **Sexcapades:** stories from a variety of women around the country who submitted their tales to us at our Happy Hook-Up research parties; via email; or via questionnaires they filled out at our website, happyhookup.com

- **Survey Says:** facts and figures from the most recent Durex Global Sex Survey, as well as final statistics tabulated from surveys submitted by men and women via our website

- **The Boys' Club Says:** insights, often crass, inane, or otherwise moronic—although occasionally insightful and uplifting—from the men around the country who submitted questionnaires via our website

- **Sexpressions:** silly little words and phrases that have found their way into our unofficial casual sex lexicon

And a final word or two of caution: Please note that this book is not intended for women who are working through any sexual dysfunctions or who have had traumatic sexual experiences. We urge you to use your good judgment and common sense and act within the context of the law in any sexual encounter. If you are faced with an unsettling situation, be as safe and responsible as possible and, if necessary, seek help from an appropriate professional—be it a therapist, medical doctor, or big, strong policeman. Do we have to add that casual sex should only be enjoyed by consenting adults? Please, tell us we don't. Oh wait, we already did. Just be careful out there!

# Introduction

Okay, girls, it's time to stop whining about your single status and start celebrating it once and for all. Why? Well, for starters, consider the fact that you don't have to answer to anyone, you can make your own rules, live according to your own agenda, and—best of all in our humble opinions—sleep with just about anyone you want. Seriously, that's a major bonus. If you were in a committed relationship, your options for intimacy would likely be a lot more limited.

Sure, sex is readily available when you can do it with your boyfriend or husband (or cheat on him if you want to go straight to hell, or at least have really bad karma)—and if you're an adventurous couple, there are all sorts of variations on the theme. But let's be honest: Most couples, particularly of the married variety, aren't up for *adventure*. They go to work, come home, eat dinner, watch a little TV and—when they're feeling really naughty and have an ounce of energy—they go at it for a few minutes before falling asleep. Pretty crazy stuff, huh? So why do so many women make finding a husband their lifelong mission? Yeah, yeah, we accept that marriage is a worthwhile pursuit, and it's got its pluses. But you? You've got options. Options!

Yes, you've got more options than you probably know what to do with. We're talking one-night stands, flings, hook-ups, friends with benefits, getting lucky—*scoring*. Call it what you want, but the bottom line is you're a far cry from "dating" like your mother did—unless you've been set up by a matchmaking service, family member, or friend (which isn't always the ideal). Until that dreamy, special someone shows up, if he ever does, you're free to embrace your sexuality and get off any way you like.

Casual sex certainly isn't anything new—but from the free love movement of the sixties to the swinging seventies to the AIDS-ridden eighties and cautiously optimistic nineties, we've come a long way, baby, and the new millennium is finding plenty of us pursuing carnal pleasures the smart and satisfying way . . . for the most part. The fact is, sex can make you feel incredible, even invincible, and the one-night stand is its purest expression—sex for the sheer sake of sex, no strings attached.

But while some women have been doing it for years, and it mostly feels great, plenty are still letting it mess with their heads *and* their hearts. Perhaps it has to do with the conflicting messages in the media and society at large. First, the sex-happy single girl is an evolved daughter of the post-sexual revolution who can sleep with whomever she wants. But when she does, along comes the old double standard: the guy is a player, the girl is a slut; the guy can remain emotionally detached, the girl can't handle guilt-free casual sex.

Meanwhile, you've got TV shows and movies portraying sexually aggressive single women . . . but by the end, they finally achieve "success" by forcing their conquests to commit. So much time is spent marrying off these people that you don't get the details, the dirt, the elusive and complicated ins and outs of no-strings-attached sex: How far should you actually go with someone you may not know all that well? Is he even worthy of you? What's the best way to handle an often uncomfortable morning after? ("Walk of shame," anyone?) How do you do it and move on without feeling guilty, slutty, used? Why would you feel that way in the first place?

That's where this book comes in. We'll talk about how to deal with all of it—getting your mind and body in the game (or maybe even out of it if the situation's not working), picking the right partner (and gracefully ditching the wrong ones), getting through the post-encounter awkwardness, and plenty of other details. We've been there, done that, and learned from the experiences, and so have the other women (and select men) profiled in these pages. The bottom line is that we want you to get what you want in the best way possible, so you can still respect *yourself* in the morning.

And while this book was written for straight, single women, when it comes to casual sex, plenty of the advice can be heeded whether you're a boy or a girl, and whether you like boys, girls, or both. We'll admit that you may actually wind up having *less* casual sex after reading what we have to say, and we suppose that's okay. If you're not comfortable with it, then by all means *don't do it*. Casual sex is not for everyone, and it doesn't have to be. Sure, you may need it more than you realize, but who are we to judge? Whatever you decide, we hope you enjoy the ride—and here's to you being ready for action.

*Are You Sure You Can,*

*and Want, to Do It?*

# Chapter One

# Got Milk?

We've all heard the old saying "He's not going to buy the cow if he's getting the milk for free"—that ubiquitous adage the aging masses (particularly our parents) throw around in a futile effort to get us to keep our pants on or at least hold out for a marriage proposal. Not only do we take exception to the implication that all women should aspire to grander and more meaningful pursuits like getting hitched—frankly, we feel a little sorry for people (women in particular) who think the one doing the milking is having all the fun or exercising all the control. The way we see it, the milker is the one doing all the work and the cow's just standing there getting off. So, the things that are wrong with this picture are many and varied.

Let's get it out of the way, right here, right now: If anyone's going to call us cows, they also need to accept that some of us just want to be milked—and we're actually enjoying it. Furthermore, not all "cows" are looking to be purchased. In fact, we prefer the more recent saying making the rounds, which goes a little something like this: "Why buy the pig just to get a little sausage?" But enough with the tired metaphors. It's not exactly a revelation that countless people, male and female alike, are comfortable having sex without a commitment in place.

Here's something that might surprise you, though. Marriage rates are at their lowest in history, and more women than ever are choosing (yes, choosing) that single status. Thirteen million unmarried women, including never-weds and divorcées, head up U.S. households, according to the 2000 census—and MarketResearch.com notes that 57 percent of those women own their own homes. Oh, and it gets better: Single women actually earn more than single men—to the tune of 28 additional cents an hour—says the Employment Policy Foundation.

Given all this, doesn't it make sense that many of us simply don't have the time to put into a relationship, let alone maintain interest in one? As renowned clinical sexologist Ava Cadell of Los Angeles told us in a recent interview, "There are plenty of women, young and mature, who are financially independent and want sex, but not a committed relationship." Emily, twenty-three, of Chapel Hill, North Carolina, agrees: "Casual sex allows you to enjoy sex without being tied down to a man that you may not necessarily be with otherwise. Being in a relationship is time consuming and draining. If you don't want the pressure of being faithful, having to call or be available, but you want sex, then make it casual." Maggie, forty, of Santa Cruz, California, adds, "Sometimes it's nice to be able to 'scratch that itch' without having to deal with the time and energy commitment of an actual relationship."

Beyond the fact that you may be too busy or independent for a relationship, there's a wealth of knowledge to be gained when you take a dip in the casual sex pool. You call the shots and do what you want, when you want, where you want, and with whom you want, and you have no one to answer to but yourself. Think of it as research: You can sample what's out there before you decide who's worthy of you, you can learn what you do and don't enjoy. We're talking major life experience here. And who wants to get involved in a serious relationship without living it up a little first?

---

**SURVEY SAYS . . .**

According to the 2003 Durex Global Sex Survey, 54 percent of Americans have had a one-night stand and 18 percent of Americans would have sex on the first night. According to our Happy Hook-Up survey, 94 percent of the women polled have had casual sex with at least one person (of those, 48 percent have had casual sex with eleven or more people).

---

Above all, casual sex is fun. It's the pleasure principle, pure and simple. "Let's face it, sex is a normal human need," says Elisha, thirty-six, of New York City. "Not everyone wants to be in a relationship just to have sex. But everyone wants sex." Perhaps this doesn't sound like a female philosophy, but believe us when we tell you, it is.

People have been allowing men to act on their sexual impulses for centuries, often arguing that it's simply a biological given—that man, by design, must spread his seed. What a crock. "One could argue that because women ovulate only once a month in contrast to the male 24/7 impregnating potential, it is women, not men, who are more inclined to have sex simply for the pleasure of it all," say Emily Kramer and Melinda Gallagher, cofounders of Cake (Cakenyc.com) in New York City, an entertainment company dedicated to providing education and information about female sexual culture. "Women have major fantasies about anonymous, no-strings-attached sex and search for positive and enjoyable sexual release. Women should not be judged for having a one-night stand, either by their partner or their peers."

# What's in a Name?

Call it what you want, but there's no way of getting around the fact that casual sex is simply commitment-free coitus. That said, some very subtle distinctions come into play on occasion. Here's the lowdown on your transient trysts, your fleeting passions, your one-off get-offs, and so on and so on:

**Booty Call** ("Who the hell would be calling me at three o'clock in the morning? Oh . . . *yeah*.") A late-night romp with someone you've met before—an acquaintance, friend, ex-boyfriend, recent hook-up. This generally transpires immediately after one party drunk dials the other.

**Fling** ("It was really, really great meeting you.") No-strings-attached action that lasts for two days or more (an excellent way to spend a holiday).

**Friends with Benefits** ("Oh my God, I so needed that.") A relationship between two people (oftentimes exes) who realize they aren't in love with each other, but why should that ruin all the fun?

**Getting Lucky** ("Thank you, good night.") Generally implies getting laid, usually by someone you just met and whom you may or may not see again (probably not). Also see "one-night stand" and "scoring."

**Hook-Up** ("This party sucks . . . wanna go for a walk?") Discreet reference to any form of intimacy from making out to heavy petting to oral sex to actual intercourse (nobody has to know how far it went if you simply say you "hooked up").

**One-Night Stand** ("Where the hell am I?") Short-lived action with someone you just met and should never expect to see again. Also see "getting lucky" and "scoring."

**Scoring** ("Yes, yes, oh yes!") Full-on sex with someone you have no interest in seeing again. Also see "getting lucky" and "one-night stand."

The bottom line: It feels good and, given the right situation, it makes you feel good about yourself. It may not be your greatest accomplishment or a skill you'd list on your résumé, but when you're doing the horizontal mambo, as Dr. Ava says, "It can boost your ego and your sexual confidence." And there's absolutely nothing wrong with that, sister. No way, no how.

Why should you give up sexual satisfaction with another person, just because you haven't found a long-term partner? "I'm single and I enjoy sex," Emily, twenty-three, of Chapel Hill, North Carolina, tells us. "I don't want to be in a relationship so it's my only outlet." Diana, thirty-one, of Chicago, offers yet another benefit: "If you're coming off a bad relationship, casual sex—maybe even with someone you would never want to date—is a good way to get back in the saddle, to get your self-esteem back on board before you start another serious relationship." Sounds good to us.

# Casual Sex Queens throughout History

As we've said, casual sex really isn't anything new. From ancient goddesses to fictional characters to today's Hollywood hotties, women have been having casual sex—even using men for their own hedonistic pleasure—for centuries. So if you find yourself without the emotional tools necessary to get it on and get gone, try channeling the carnal appetites and attitudes of these fine femme fatales.

**Aphrodite,** a.k.a. Venus to the Romans, was the Greek goddess from whose name "aphrodisiac" is derived. While often called virginal, that really meant she was fabulously independent. Her priestesses weren't actual virgins, either—they were more like her single-girl posse. Aphrodite got knocked up after having sex with a mortal, Anchises, and gave birth to the Trojan War hero, Aeneas. (Isn't it ironic? Apparently Trojan wasn't making condoms yet.)

**Tallulah Bankhead,** a contemporary of Greta Garbo and Marlene Dietrich, has been quoted as saying, "The only reason I went to Hollywood was to fuck that divine Gary Cooper." She also told *Motion Picture* magazine in 1932, "I haven't had an affair for six months. Six months! Too long . . . If there's anything the matter with me now, it's not Hollywood or Hollywood's state of mind . . . the matter with me is, I want a man! . . . six months is a long, long while. I want a man!" Another wonderful quotable and we'll call it a day for Tallulah: "It's the good girls that keep the diaries. The bad girls never have the time." Amen, Tallulah.

**Mae West,** whose famous line, "Why don't you come up and see me sometime?" from the 1933 film *She Done Him Wrong*, sure shook up the twenties and thirties, and not just with her stage or screen personas. She was known to have had plenty of affairs and the tougher the guy, the better—although she did once admit, "I go for two kinds of men: the kind with muscles and the kind without." She even went to jail for ten days for "corrupting the morals of youth" because of her controversial vaudeville show "Sex" in 1925. As Mae once said, "I used to be Snow White, but I drifted."

**Mary Richards:** As much as the writers for *The Mary Tyler Moore Show* wanted us to believe that Mary Richards was as pure as the driven Minneapolis snow, we'd beg to differ. Throughout the run of the show Mary "dated"—a lot. We can't say that she hooked up with all those men (she also expertly ditched the losers), but we will point out that during the show's seven-year run, twenty-five men guest-starred in her life (that's not including Lou Grant and his affection for her). In season three, her parents arrived at her apartment one morning only to discover that Mary had spent the night at a man's house. Hmm . . . we never did see that guy again. Scandalous!

**Madonna:** Yes, she's settled down now and is a loving wife and devoted mother, but let's flash back to the early days of her career, when she claimed to be the original "boy toy" and wore that statement emblazoned proudly on her person. She spent the next few years shocking the public with her in-your-face sexuality, whether she was writhing around on a bed on stage, making out with men and women in her videos, or releasing the infamous *Sex* book. Nope, this girl was nothing "like a virgin." In fact, she's been quoted as saying, "Losing my virginity was a career move."

**Samantha Jones,** the fictional *Sex and the City* character portrayed on television by Kim Cattral, made "funky spunk" a household expression (okay, in certain households) and had no problem celebrating her proclivity for promiscuity. We saw her jump from one bed—and man—to another. The self-proclaimed "bad girl" of the hit television show knew what she wanted and always got it. Here's to her.

**Christina Aguilera** told *Zoo Magazine* in January 2004, "I have casual sex, I love casual sex." She went on to ask, "What is so wrong with a twenty-two-year-old woman showing her sexuality? If people want to insult me, let them. Call me a slag [British slang for a prostitute]. If being a slag means being a strong woman, I'll gladly be that." We were never too sure whether to support this pop tart or not—until now.

**Angelina Jolie** admitted in March 2004 that she enjoys casual sex in the "friends with benefits" category: "I went for about two years with absolutely no man around me and then decided to get closer to men who were already very close friends of mine," she told the *New York Post.* "It's kind of an adult way of having adult relationships . . . Meeting a man in a hotel room for a few hours and then going back and putting my son to bed and not seeing that man again for a few months is about what I can handle now . . . I can feel like a woman and get close to a man, but it's not a relationship that interferes with my family . . . I've never had a one-night stand in my life—these are people that I know very well." Talk about breaking the rules and making your own. If only she could explain that whole marrying Billy Bob thing to us . . . hopefully, her casual conquests are a lot hotter and a lot less creepy. We hear they are.

Of course, for every woman who may love casual sex, there will be one who may not—and we'll be the first to admit that it's not for everyone. After all, it's hammered into the heads of most girls from the time we're born that we're supposed to be in a relationship or that "true love waits," "good girls wait," or that sex is something serious, perhaps even *dirty*, and that women above all other creatures can't (and shouldn't) have sex without being in love. All of these ideas that have been shoved down our throats for so long aren't just a lot to swallow but a lot to digest, let alone transcend.

Therefore, the first order of business in this whole casual sex game is figuring out if you've bought into these messages. Are you a "good girl?" (Or have you been a very bad girl?) Are you a woman that gets wrapped up in the what-ifs and the could-bes? (Or do you just want to get off?) Do you have a serious streak of romantic idealism? (Or are you all about the cock?) Would you give anything to have a relationship right now? (Or do you cringe at the mention of commitment?) Honestly, there's nothing wrong with wanting more. As we've said, plenty of people would like to get married eventually, and that's totally legitimate. You've just got to be honest with yourself about what your wants and needs are at this very moment.

So close your eyes, tap into your deepest, most passionate inner voice, and ask yourself this question: "Can I have sex without being in love—without even having a commitment in place—and not get emotionally attached?" If you're not getting a clear answer, look back on your past sexual experiences. (If you haven't had any, check your driver's license and make sure you're over the age of eighteen. If you are, you may proceed.) What compels you to be with a man? Do you automatically picture a future with most guys you meet? Whatever it may be, really figure out what's come up for you when getting together with someone. If you're not sure that you can be the kind of woman who doesn't get too attached, who simply seeks pleasure for pleasure's sake, if you're skeptical that that kind of woman even exists—well, meet Sheridan:

## SEXCAPADE: Losin' It

*I lost my virginity in my early twenties, which I know is pretty late by just about anyone's standards—including mine. But I'm actually glad I waited that long. I was pretty clear on what I wanted by the time I met the first guy I slept with—and at that point, all I wanted was some action and to finally have sex.*

*I was working at a radio station, and one night, I went to see a band from England that my coworker Tanya had interviewed on the morning show. After the band's set, a couple of the guys came over to chat with me and Tanya, and I found myself starting to flirt heavily with Colin, the bass player. It was fun talking to someone so quick-witted and charming who seemed to think I was just as funny and adorable as he was.*

*After a few beers at a couple of different bars, Tanya and I were invited back to the band's hotel. When we got there, Tanya and the guitarist left to find the hot tub, and Colin and I weren't far behind. We all stripped to our underwear, got in, and as Tanya got down with her man on one side, Colin and I began our own little lust-fest across the whirlpool. After a* while, Colin asked if I wanted go back to the room. Not exactly a tough decision. So we got out, dried ourselves off with our clothes, and made a mad dash back to the building.

Within minutes, we were having sex; in retrospect, it was one of the best sexual experiences of my life (which I find amazing, considering it was my first time). We hung out in bed for a while afterwards, but since I had to work that morning and the sun was starting to come up, I told Colin I'd better head out. I got dressed, he walked me to the hotel lobby to get a taxi, and I was on my way. We did exchange addresses and stayed in touch for the next several months. He actually came back into town about a year later, at which point I'd racked up some more experience, and we had about a month or two of no-strings-attached sex, which just got better every time.

For the next ten years or so, I actively pursued just about any guy I found attractive and almost always wound up having really great sex. I felt really empowered each time that I had a one-night stand. I had a couple of relationships along the way, but I also realized this was my time to sow my oats—to enjoy myself without all the issues and effort that come with some-thing more serious.

I'm involved in a monogamous relationship now, and it's going really well. I'm just about ready to settle down, but I look back on all of my experiences pretty fondly. I'm glad I had them—no regrets.

—Sheridan, thirty-four, Los Angeles

And there you have it. Some women can absolutely have sex without wanting anything more. They even seek it out, and it ends there. The key is to keep your emotions and expectations in check (in truth: altogether absent). As Sheridan told us: "I know a lot of girls who say they want to sleep around, but they get too involved in the whole thing. I've had friends come up to me a day or two after having a one-night stand and ask how they should deal with the fact that the guy hasn't called yet. I tell them: 'Don't expect him to . . . you shouldn't even want him to.'"

But how do you get into that head-space? As many of our friends have asked us: How can we, as women, have sex and not feel something more? Well, first you've got to figure out your predominant emotional identity. And to help you, we've come up with a little quiz (don't worry—it's a fun one) to help you gauge your psychological readiness and avoid any wounded feelings after the deed is done. So before you do that guy, check your head with our Sexual Aptitude Test (S.A.T.):

## The Sexual Aptitude Test (S.A.T.)

1. Your idea of the perfect chick-flick double feature is

    A. *Young Guns* and *Chocolat*. (Mmmm, Emilio Estevez, Kiefer Sutherland, Lou Diamond Phillips, Charlie Sheen . . . and Johnny Depp!)

    B. *When Harry Met Sally* and *Hope Floats*. (Mmmm, old friends become lovers and get married!)

    C. *Heathers* and *Cruel Intentions*. (Mmmm, hot sex with Christian Slater and Ryan Phillippe!)

    D. *Good Will Hunting* and *A Beautiful Mind*. (Mmmm, Matt Damon and Russell Crowe are so smart!)

2. The main quality you look for in a guy you want to sleep with is

    A. intelligence.

    B. sexual skill.

    C. appearance.

    D. sense of humor.

3. You believe that premarital sex is okay, as long as

    A. the people involved have discussed it first.

    B. the people involved truly love each other.

    C. the people involved are totally horny.

    D. the people involved are totally hot.

4. Your ultimate celebrity fantasy involves

    A. you, Tom Cruise, and lots of fooling around.

    B. you, Tom Hanks, and lots of laughing and cuddling.

    C. you, Tom Robbins, and lots of literary pontificating.

    D. you, Tommy Lee, and lots of hot sex.

5. How many sexual partners have you had in your life?

    A. 0

    B. 1–5

    C. 6–10

    D. 11–plus

6. Your attitude toward guys and condoms is

    A. you always try to make him see the practical reasons for using one.

    B. you know he should wear one, but you feel bad making him.

    C. it's easy to make him use one if you make it part of the foreplay.

    D. no condom, no sex.

7. Your friends would probably describe you as

    A. sleek and stylish.

    B. seriously smart.

    C. hypersexual.

    D. hypersensitive.

8. You would only marry a guy after determining that

    A. you're intellectually compatible.

    B. you're emotionally compatible.

    C. you're sexually compatible.

    D. you're genetically compatible (what cute kids!).

9. When you think of the ultimate woman, you think

    A. Madonna.

    B. Oprah Winfrey.

    C. Mother Teresa.

    D. Pam Anderson.

10. The *Sex and the City* character with whom you most identified was

    A. Carrie—a looks-conscious lover.

    B. Samantha—a serious sex goddess.

    C. Charlotte—a hopeless romantic.

    D. Miranda—a cerebral seductress.

# Scoring (No, Not That Kind—At Least, Not Yet)

Calculate your points according to the following key:

1. A = 120
   B = 20
   C = 160
   D = 80

2. A = 80
   B = 160
   C = 120
   D = 20

3. A = 80
   B = 20
   C = 160
   D = 120

4. A = 120
   B = 20
   C = 80
   D = 160

5. A = 20
   B = 80
   C = 120
   D = 160

6. A = 80
   B = 20
   C = 120
   D = 160

7. A = 120
   B = 80
   C = 160
   D = 20

8. A = 80
   B = 20
   C = 160
   D = 120

9. A = 160
   B = 80
   C = 20
   D = 120

10. A = 120
    B = 160
    C = 20
    D = 80

# Based upon Your Score, You Are:

### 200–500: Sappy

You're a nice, sweet girl. You also tend to be romantically idealistic and your experiences with sex may be fairly limited, if not altogether absent. Because finding Mr. Right is likely to be pretty high on your list of priorities, casual sex probably isn't for you. If you're absolutely hell-bent on having a one-night stand, read on and then reexamine your disposition. If you continue to come up with the same score after repeated attempts, you should probably dismiss the notion of having casual sex altogether. It's just too dirty and complicated!

### 501–1,000: Smart

Congratulations, you are the sharpest tool in the shed. Just be aware that when it comes to casual sex—not to mention most things in life—you have a tendency to overthink the situation. Therefore, you're going to need to make sure to wrap your head around the fact that hooking up is not love. You might also consider reading every study done on the art of the female orgasm and having a good, long chat about your intentions with your prospective screw before doing him (for more on that matter, read on). You know what you want, and you probably know how to get it. You just might wind up thinking you want more than he does (or vice versa); you're so analytical that way.

### 1,001–1,400: Sassy

You are definitely in touch with your libido. You're lookin' good, because—no disrespect intended—you're shallow enough to want a guy for his body only. Just make sure you don't fall in love with his Adonis-like good looks. It's happened to the best of us, as you'll see in some of the stories that follow.

**1,401–1,600: Slutalicious**

You are clearly ready for your one-night stand. You have the experience, the intentions, the perspective, and the hedonistic passion. You are completely okay with using a man for sex and nothing more, so you're pretty much good to go. (But keep reading—you're not home free yet, honey.)

Okay, then—how did you do? Are you in the right head-space for a good, hard roll in the hay, or do you need to work on a few of the finer points before doing the deed? Hopefully, what you're coming to realize is that to successfully enjoy casual sex, you've got to make sure that you're approaching it with the optimum attitude and perspective, that you're having it because it's what you want—and *all* you want. You've got to do it for good, noncommittal fun—not because you're hoping that sleeping with the guy will make him want you more; not because you're seeking a quick cure for painfully low self-esteem; not because you're looking for Mr. Right. As Dr. Ava told us, "A woman must give herself permission to enjoy sexual pleasure without having any emotional expectations. Realize that you can have lovers who satisfy your physical needs without needing any other kind of attachment."

No matter how you scored on your S.A.T., though, even we'll admit there's a lot more to being emotionally equipped than simply wanting to get laid. Take, for instance, the story of Andrea:

## SEXCAPADE: Lust to Love

*As my twenty-seventh birthday was approaching, I decided to throw a party for myself and invite all the single guys I knew (in addition to my friends, of course). In the two years since my last serious relationship (which completely broke my heart), I'd been having my fair share of one-night stands. You know what they say: the best way to get over a man is with another man. So I got over—and under—and next to—plenty of them. I was actually starting to enjoy using men for sex.*

*But I had my eye on one guy in particular: Evan. He was a singer in a band, and some mutual friends had introduced us a couple of years before. Even though I always tried to play it cool when we were around each other, there was this intense chemistry between us. So when I ran into Evan the week before my party, I invited him to the festivities, and he said he'd love to come.*

*I actually kind of forgot Evan was going to be there, as the night wore on and he still hadn't shown up; there were plenty of other guys there to help me celebrate, and I was sure I'd be hooking up with someone. But then, there he was—bleached blonde hair, six feet tall, piercing blue eyes, incredible rocker-boy style. I couldn't even look at any of the other guys; I tried to pretend to flirt with a couple of them to make Evan jealous, but that lasted about two minutes. I couldn't wait to get back to him. As we chatted, the sparks were flying. He was so quick with the comebacks, and I was too. I could tell he was getting off on talking to me.*

*More and more people began to leave the party, and pretty soon, it was just me and Evan and a couple of our friends. When the others left the room, Evan immediately pressed up against me, and we started making out. It was seriously hot. I mean, this guy was incredibly gorgeous, we'd been flirting with each other for such a long time, and it was obvious to me that we were desperate for each other.*

When our friends walked in on us making out, we didn't even notice—and thankfully they were just coming in to tell us they had to leave. Needless to say, we couldn't get them out the door fast enough. And then, we couldn't get our clothes off fast enough. It was one of the most amazing nights of my life. This guy really knew how to get me off; we did it in the bedroom, the hallway, the living room, the bathroom. I felt incredible.

The next morning, Evan took off pretty early. He got my phone number and said he'd call. I didn't expect to care much about whether or not I heard from him—after all, I'd slept with another guy just a week before, so I was in that sort of "on to the next one" mentality. But the truth is that I couldn't wait to talk to Evan or see him again. The next day, when I mentioned to our mutual friends that he'd spent the night, one of them told me Evan had been asking about me off and on for the past couple of years . . . and that got my hopes up even higher. Then, my mind just started racing—where we could go on our next date, how we would spend our weekends, what we would name our kids. Of course, I wasn't that serious about him yet, but I was so excited to have finally found a guy that I really thought was worth more than a fling. This could be my new boyfriend.

Unfortunately, Evan waited three days to call me, and I knew the games were just beginning. I called him on his "three-day rule" phone call, and he acted oblivious. I kept telling myself not to get emotionally attached, but the few times we talked and hung out after my birthday, he led me to believe that he was interested in more; we even talked about how we were both tired of sleeping around and how we really wanted to find something more serious. But, after a few weeks,

*I stopped hearing from him altogether. I'm sure he got spooked, he just wasn't ready—or, worse still, maybe he just wasn't into me for anything more than sex.*

*I was pretty destroyed, but I also wised up. I had learned my lesson, and knew I had to get back out there and meet some new people. Within a few weeks, I was back in the swing of things. I met a guy who was cute but not very bright, and we fooled around a few times. Then, I met another guy who was really hot, but so obviously a player that I didn't even think about pursuing him for anything more serious (in fact, he pursued me, and I just blew him off). I began to realize that if I was going to sleep with someone, I needed to make sure he didn't have the whole package to offer, so I wouldn't get so sprung on him. And when I finally did meet a guy who was everything I wanted, I actually refrained from sleeping with him right away ... and proceeded with caution.*

—Andrea, twenty-nine, Portland, Oregon

Here we have one of the biggest snags that comes with sleeping around, and the one that winds up biting even the most independent-minded women in the butt: thinking you just want to get some action but then realizing you really want more than that. Andrea was *almost* in the right head-space: a single woman who didn't necessarily want, nor have time for, a total commitment. As she told us, "I really wasn't looking for a relationship. But when I finally got the opportunity to be with Evan, and I got the impression that he wanted more, and I was so painfully attracted to him, it wound up hurting more than I expected it to." Yes, it's a little bit sad, but it's something even smart, evolved, empowered women like Andrea experience.

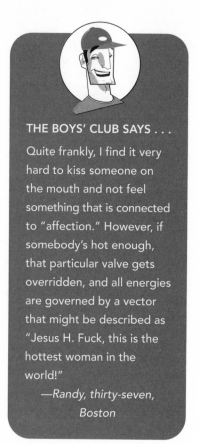

It's not that Evan did anything wrong, and neither did Andrea. A lot of guys are just looking for a little action, as are a lot of girls, and both Evan and Andrea started off being pretty clear, albeit unspoken, about that fact. But Andrea forgot that as much as she kept her emotions in check going into the situation, she also needed to make sure that she kept them in check coming *out* of the encounter. (Repeat after us: *This is just sex. This is just sex. This is just sex.*)

In essence, Andrea lost control of the situation. Case in point: She was initially the one pursuing Evan, but when she gave him her number, she put the ball in his court and put herself in a vulnerable position. Halley, thirty-eight, of Denver, notes that it often has a lot to do with how experienced you are: "When I was in my twenties, I was very insecure and, I think, while I was learning about sex, I was also feeding my ego. My self-worth was wrapped up in getting the guy to sleep with me. I was always disappointed if he didn't want it to go further. As I grew older and wiser, I was able to take what I wanted from the experience, be satisfied, and not expect more. I became the controller of my sex life, not the guy."

We'll get to this in greater detail later, but for now, suffice to say that in order to remain in emotional control, you need to be the director—you lead, he follows, and rarely, if ever, should it be the other way around.

## SEXPRESSIONS

**dicknotize,** v., to become obsessed with a man, particularly after having sex with him.

e.g., "I don't know what the hell happened to me last night—I think Andrew dicknotized me 'cause now I can't stop thinking about him."

What we all need to realize is that it's pretty easy to become psychologically attached when you've scored a guy who might have even more to offer than the high hard one. The biggest problem with the Evan and Andrea debacle was that Andrea was already looking at Evan in more than just a casual way. As she learned, even if all you want to do is knock them boots, that doesn't mean you won't be going for it with a guy who winds up being more than you ever imagined—smart, funny, and a great conversationalist, not to mention damn sexy. Of course, you'd like to get this veritable demigod into bed, but it's unlikely you'll just want it to be a one-off encounter.

What to do? Figure out if he's going to have you hot for something more serious than no-strings-attached sex *before* you go any further. You can start by assessing the situation according to the following checklist.

# Is He a One-Night Man?

Place a check mark next to each of the following questions to which your answer is "yes."

❏ Is he a friend or close acquaintance?

❏ Have you bonded heavily?

❏ Do you know his first and last name?

❏ Does he know *your* first and last name?

❏ Do you know what he does for a living?

❏ Does he know what *you* do for a living?

❏ Do you care about or respect what he does for a living?

❏ Have you thought about how your first name and his last name sound together?

❏ Have you fantasized about where your honeymoon will be?

❏ Have you pictured him fathering your children?

The more "yes" answers to the questions above, the less likely this is just sex. As we've said, there's nothing wrong with wanting a serious relationship—but if that's what you're after, hooking up is probably not going to be for you.

---

SEXPRESSIONS

**playa,** *n.,* a guy who sleeps around—or, when pronounced with a Spanish accent, a beach

e.g., "He's such a playa—I saw him get together with three different women down in Playa Blanca, Mexico, and that was in one night."

At this point, if you've determined you're in the right head-space for something casual, and your prospective conquest has passed the test and been deemed a one-night man, things are looking good and you're almost ready to proceed with the action. However, relationship experts and sex therapists alike say it might be worth your while to make sure that all the cards are on the table—that your intentions, as well as his, are perfectly clear, and that no one's going to be coming back begging for more. "You have to be able to communicate by saying something like, 'I want you to be my perfect lover, but I don't want to fall in love. Can you handle that?'" says Dr. Ava. "Most men will jump at the chance to have sex with a woman who makes a statement like that." Perhaps it *should* be obvious to you both at this point, and if it is, great. But don't be too sure. Take Patty's story, for instance:

## SEXCAPADE: Take It Like a Man

*One Friday night, I went out to a restaurant across the street from my office with a few of the girls—the same place we usually went to celebrate another workweek being done. Around eight o'clock, happy hour turned into dinner, and over walked Mike—our very cute and very young waiter—who I'd had my eye on for weeks. "Back again?" Mike said to us, and then proceeded to flirt shamelessly, with me in particular.*

*As dinner continued, the conversation at our table turned to sex toys, and my friend Rachel told us about one called "the Rabbit" recently popularized on an episode of Sex and the City. I won't claim I've never owned or operated a vibrator, but I'd just got out of a seven-year marriage, and I was a little out* of the loop. My ex-husband wasn't very adventurous, so I had long since retired my college toys. When the girls heard that, they decided that after dinner, we would have to head to the sex shop located conveniently around the corner.

We were paying up when Mike came over and started clearing the table. It was so cute the way he was picking up the plates and shooting me sweet and flirty looks. I really wanted to slip him my number but was way too embarrassed to do it in front of my friends, so I just smiled seductively and said good night.

My friends and I arrived at the sex shop, where there was plenty of giggling and a whole lot of "been there, tried that" among us. I decided I would take Rachel's advice and get the Rabbit. I was trying to figure out which color would match my bed linens when I felt someone walk up behind me. I turned around, and there was Mike. He was out of his uniform and in a cowboy shirt and jeans. "I don't think you'll need that tonight," he said. "No?" I replied. "I guess I won't."

I don't generally pick up men, especially ones as young as I figured Mike was, but I decided, what the hell; you only live once. I started thinking about how I could teach him a few tricks, and he could practice them on me with all the zeal and staying power of a twenty-one-year-old. Plus I was impressed that he'd followed me, and the thought of getting off with a man suddenly sounded a lot more appealing than a toy. Mike and I ducked out the back, and I phoned Rachel's cell to let her know what had happened. She said she "totally got it" and hoped I would too (bad pun intended).

Since my place was closer than Mike's (and given the intensity we were going at), that's where we headed. We barely made it in the door before our clothes were off. But afterwards, having got what I wanted, I just wanted Mike gone. I didn't want to deal with the morning-after pleasantries—but I also felt bad booting him out. So against my better judgment, I let him spend the night. *Mistake number one.*

When we woke up, the first words out of Mike's mouth were, "Good morning, sleepyhead! I was just thinking it would be fun to see a movie tonight . . . or I can cook you dinner . . . or maybe both!" My reply: "I need coffee . . . now. My head is killing me." To which he said, "I can make you some coffee . . . or we could go get brunch." By then I was halfway down the hall, trying to figure out a way to get him out the door. I rushed around, claiming I had too much to do and wasn't going to have any time.

In the taxi, on the way back to pick up our cars, he asked for my number. I wanted to say, "Last night was great and fun, but that's all it was. I don't see this going any further." But instead I gave him my cell number and a quick kiss good-bye; I figured I would avoid answering the phone for a few days, and he would eventually get the point. *Mistake number two.*

My cell phone rang the whole weekend. I got three mushy voice mails, and on Monday morning, there were flowers on my desk with a card that read, "What a great evening! What a connection! Can't wait to see you again. Love, Mike." Evening? Connection? Love?! I had to nip this one in the bud. I didn't want to hurt his feelings, but we were obviously *not on the same page—and the fact that he worked right across the street from my office and knew exactly how to find me was a little scary.*

*I stopped by Mike's restaurant after work to talk to him, but the second I walked in, he gave me a big hug and kiss and introduced me to his boss as his "new gal Patty." I didn't know what to do. We small-talked for a bit, and I mentioned that my birthday was on Wednesday and I was crazy busy at work, so I couldn't make definite plans that week. Mistake number three. By six o'clock on Wednesday, Mike had called three times, sung "Happy Birthday" twice, and sent flowers to my office and my home.*

*That night, I poured a large glass of wine and prepped myself for the phone call. I told him I had just come out of a seven-year marriage and didn't want to be in a relationship— I needed my freedom—and that he was a really sweet guy, but we wanted different things. I must say, he was really great about it. After we hung up, I felt like a huge weight had been lifted. I just wish I'd been honest from the start. Thankfully, my friends got me the Rabbit as a birthday gift.*

—Patty, thirty-seven, Newport Beach, California

Just when you thought it was safe to go back in the dating pool, along comes Mike. This isn't just an example of the role reversal that can and does happen between the sexes; it is also evidence of how things can unravel if everyone's intentions aren't made crystal clear, right out of the gate. If you know that you're only interested in no-strings-attached action, as Dr. Ava said, you might want to let him know that and make sure he feels the same way. If it seems like oversharing, and too much talk is going to kill the mood, use your judgment, but don't underestimate the value of a quick, "just so we're clear" conversation. It might be the best possible way to ensure you both get what you came for (so to speak).

# The Last Word on Getting Your Head in the Game

Can *you* have casual sex? It's possible—but grasping all of the following concepts will make it a lot more likely on an emotional level.

### Understand That Sex Is Not Love

For many people—male and female alike—this is a tough distinction to make. If you're one of those people, casual sex is unlikely to be in the cards for you. It's true that sex can be amazing when it's with someone you love—but is it always? No. And the same goes for sex with someone you don't love—it can be incredible or incredibly disappointing. Sex and love are often two distinct entities. Believe this to be true, and see what unfolds. If you can't, as we said, simply don't have casual sex. Be honest with yourself about your thoughts on the matter and your own moral code.

### Keep Your Emotions and Your Orgasms Separate

To do this, you need to have enough self-awareness (and probably age and experience) to understand what you want from the situation and why you want it. Again, you must gauge the situation and be clear and honest with yourself before doing the deed. You might even want to quickly contemplate how you might feel after the fact—ask yourself if you're sure that you'll be able to walk away without wanting to see him again.

## THE BOYS' CLUB SAYS ...

If you really want to enjoy casual sex—well, let's put it this way—you are there to watch a Hong Kong action movie, not an Ingmar Bergman picture. So do not expect from the swordplay and the gun battles and the Mexican standoffs and the carnage what you would get from an Ingmar Bergman picture—which is to say an exploration of the dark night of the human soul. Just enjoy the arterial spray.

—Tom, thirty-four, Santa Monica, California

## Believe in the Pleasure Principle

Focus on your own gratification, on a purely physical level, and make the encounter about what gets you off. If pleasing him does that, then please him. If you'd like him to do something he's not, ask for it. A successful hook-up is when you feel completely satisfied and happy with yourself.

## Make Sure It's Just Sex

As previously noted, go for a guy who doesn't have the whole package—perhaps just the below-the-belt package. Be clear about your expectations and his, if necessary. Don't spend too much time bonding with each other before or after the fact. "If one engages in casual sex, one must understand that they are meeting a need and not simulating feelings of love. If one begins to cuddle, to share life experiences, one will begin to develop attachments to the sex partner," says Jewel, forty-one, of Long Beach, California. So limit your conversations with him to the here and now. This can include shameless flirting, observations about what's going on around you, or your thoughts on sex and sexuality. Try not to discuss too much about your past or future—or his. That said, it never hurts to casually enquire about his sexual history. You can do this in a flirtatious way that makes the conversation hot but also helps you gauge what risks might be involved (see chapter 2 for more on this). Then, focus on the action and the action alone.

## Limit the Encounters

The more times you see a person, the longer you spend together, the greater your expectations will be. "I abide by the 'no more than three times rule' because I firmly believe that after the third time, somebody will develop feelings. Keep it simple, easy and painless," says Emily, twenty-three, of Chapel Hill, North Carolina. Isabel, thirty-four, of Atlanta, agrees: "Casual sex, for me, would have to take place with the same person over a shorter time span. If this is a repeat process, one person is going to develop feelings and get hurt. Keep it short and sweet."

## Break the Rules

We've already discussed the whole double standard that often exists when it comes to men who sleep around versus women who do. So, here's the deal: We, as females, need to show the world that sex without commitment is absolutely our prerogative. You can call us every name in the book for doing it, but those labels will only make us stronger. In fact, embrace those labels. Say, "I'm a slut! I'm a whore! I love sex!" and mean it. "Society around us needs to change and begin to encourage women to find pleasure—pleasure for pleasure's sake," say Emily Kramer and Melinda Gallagher, cofounders of Cake. "The one-night stand is not inherently a negative or a male experience. It is possible for women to have a pleasurable, responsible, and safe one-night stand. Have no fear—cultural norms will catch up with us if we give them no choice."

## Assert Your Power

The important thing is to make sure that you're the one calling the shots—or, at least, that it's a mutual thing. Do not let a guy decide he's scored you—it should always be completely equal on both sides. Operate this way and perhaps, ultimately, women will be accepted as being as sexual as men, the stigma will dissipate, and the labels will lose their meaning altogether. Hey, a girl can dream . . .

## Own Your Sexuality

Before you have a casual encounter, get to know your body. Masturbate. Maybe even watch pornography. Know what turns you on and what doesn't. Figure out what you want from a sexual encounter and what you don't. Above all, understand that your body is capable of amazing things and can be the source of tremendous pleasure for yourself and for someone else. Don't be shy when it comes to receiving pleasure. If he's not pressing the right buttons, tell him or, better yet, gently guide him there. "Tell him what turns you on," says Dr. Ava. "Most men will take direction quite well. Say something like, 'I have the best orgasms when I'm receiving oral sex.'" When you embrace your sexuality, you'll be able to enjoy a casual encounter, not to mention a more serious sexual relationship. "The more time women spend developing our own sexuality and our own confidence with giving and getting pleasure, the better our sex life becomes, period," say Kramer and Gallagher.

## Keep Yourself Busy

Before you can get caught up in Mr. Last Night, start looking for Mr. Tonight. Go down the list of men you've had your eye on. Don't dismiss the value of occupying yourself with all the other things in your life, either: throw yourself into your job, a hobby, a class, things around the house—anything that will take your mind off yesterday's man. The more you focus on the here and now (devoid of the dude you just did), the less likely you'll obsess over him.

## Bond with the Girls

It's incredible how easy it is to forget a guy (especially ones who are only good for one thing) when you're interacting with friends with whom you're more deeply connected. Furthermore, they'll be there for you if you want to discuss what transpired with your latest conquest—and they'll be ready with advice, perspective, and a big bottle of celebratory wine.

So there it is. Casual sex is largely about attitude—the *right* attitude—and that means a clear understanding of what you want and what he wants, too. Focus exclusively on having one great night with the guy, and don't let your thoughts go anywhere near entertaining what's going to happen next, whether or not he's going to call you, want you, and be your everything. It's just not going to happen, honey. At least, don't expect it to. Stay in control—before, during, after—and then accept that that's it. Finito. The end. Flip him over, he's done.

*The Less Sexy Side of*

*Doing the Deed*

*Chapter Two*

# Herpes and Scabies and Crabs, Oh My!

f you've made it this far, we're betting on the fact that you are indeed a woman on a mission—a girl who, more power to you, wants to get laid and feels confident that you can keep your emotions and expectations in check. You've admitted it to yourself and you'll admit it to anyone else: You're going to be getting some and, though you don't want to be overconfident or jinx your chances, if all goes well, it will be soon. You're not thinking about meeting the man you'll grow old with—just the man you'll get bold with. But are you ready? No, are you *really* ready?

Part of the excitement of having casual sex may be the spur-of-the-moment spontaneity, but not everything has to be totally unexpected. In fact, chances are you're going to feel a lot better about a number of things if you think first and take care of the serious business before the deed goes down. Up first: protect yourself, especially your health.

# Shake the Disease

Uh oh—it's only chapter 2, and here we go already: Sex kills! Of course, the alarmist tactics didn't work on us either. But the bottom line is: have sex with someone you don't know (or, to be perfectly honest, have sex, period), and you increase your chances of contracting a sexually transmitted (venereal) disease or infection—also known as an STD or STI. The more partners you have, the better your odds (or worse the outlook).

Some of these super fun infections aren't curable, some can leave you with lifelong struggles, health problems, possibly infertility—and yes, even death. We don't mean to harsh your mellow, but we can't really go any further—and neither should you—without considering the risks. We don't say this to scare; we say this because we care and, yes, because we've been there.

We know you've heard it a million times, to the point where you're tired of hearing it: carry a condom with you, never have sex (especially casual sex) without a condom—and don't forget those ever-popular dental dams for your cunnilingual activities—ad infinitum. We know it's redundant. Perhaps it's tired. Maybe it's a pain in the butt. But, guess what? It's the most important advice you can follow. And even latex won't keep you disease free in all instances, just as not all casual encounters are going to leave you infected or diseased. All we're saying is that if you're aware of the possibilities, you'll be more likely to make sure that whatever happens is as clean and protected as possible. Consider the experiences of Lydia:

## SEXCAPADE: I Got It Bad

*I like sex a lot, I really do. But, I've got to say, I think my body tries to tell me something almost every time I do it. The first one-night stand I ever had was with a German guy I met while I was traveling around Europe. We met late one night at a club, and we did it on the living-room floor of a flat he was sharing with four other guys. We used condoms—we were careful. It was a good time, but my most vivid memory is of sleeping under this thin little blanket, no heat on in the place, and I spent most of the night freezing my ass off. I couldn't wait to get out of there. And when I did, the next morning, I was wishing I'd seen the place with the lights on. It was a mess—a scary, nasty, filthy mess.*

*A week or so later, back in the States, I woke up itching like crazy down below. I did my best to examine myself and actually pulled something off of my pubic area. I held it between my fingers and gazed down at this tiny thing with little white legs wiggling around in the light. Jesus Christ! I was in my car and over to the hospital in no time. Yup, I had one seriously scary case of crabs. I was mortified when I went into the emergency room and told the doctor the situation. I'm sure they see it all the time, and in retrospect, I guess it was kind of funny that I went to the emergency room at all—but I just wanted those things gone.*

*The doctor gave me some medicated shampoo and I was on my way. When I got home, I stripped the bed and threw the* sheets in the washer—hot water, lots of bleach. Then I ran to the shower and after scrubbing for what seemed like hours, I decided the razor was a better option. I've kept my pubic hair completely shaved off ever since then. It's been worth it. I vacuumed the hell out of the house that night, too. I swear I almost called in an exterminator to tent the place.

I held off on having sex for a while after that. But a girl can't live on masturbation alone (at least not this one). The next few times I had casual sex, I kept getting bladder infections. The thing about bladder infections is that when I take the antibiotics for them, I get a yeast infection too. I once had a bladder infection, a yeast infection, and my period all at the same time. That was not pretty.

More recently, a routine Pap came back abnormal. For a moment there, it looked like I had HPV and, the more I learned about it, the more I realized this could potentially kill me. It turned out to be a false positive, but it freaked me out. If it had been HPV and I hadn't been diagnosed in time, it could have led to cervical cancer. Cancer from sex—who knew? Not me, though I sure as hell should have.

While none of these problems has been fun, I've had a pretty good time with almost every guy I've been with. Not everyone has been worth a visit to the doctor, but they have helped me to figure out better and smarter ways to approach sex going forward. I never leave the house without condoms and I'm religious about getting tested annually for STDs. I'm just a lot more careful now. And being careful has never made the experience less enjoyable—if anything, it's made it better.

—Lydia, thirty-eight, Houston

## Reality Check-Up

No doubt about it: If you're having casual sex, there's one nonnegotiable: Get a Pap test annually. The American Cancer Society estimated that more than ten thousand women would develop invasive cervical cancer in 2004 alone, and nearly four thousand women would die from it in the same year. Certain strains of human papillomavirus (HPV; see appendix 2) are considered the primary risk factor for cervical cancer; the only surefire way to catch HPV early, and prevent it from progressing to a life-threatening point, is to get tested. In fact, over half of women with newly diagnosed cervical cancer had not had a Pap smear in five years. By early detection of abnormal cells, regular Pap smears reduce the risk of invasive cervical cancer.

Also, to avoid serious complications, seek an early diagnosis and treatment at the first sign of any STD symptoms. Talk to your doctor about having a routine STD screening as part of your annual physical or gynecological exam, since many STDs have no symptoms. Note that STD screenings are not necessarily part of your annual gynecological exam and that Pap smears do not screen for STDs other than HPV. Furthermore, even if a screening comes back negative, you aren't necessarily in the clear. Tests aren't always completely accurate, and some STDs don't show up immediately—yet another reason to be as careful as possible and have regular exams.

# Don't Catch Me If You Can

Not only should you use condoms (and dental dams), but you should be aware of your surroundings and even pay attention to any telling signs from the person you're considering having sex with (not that symptoms are always readily apparent). Lydia was informed enough to know some of the risks, but she also told us that she wasn't entirely aware of all of the things she could contract. She knew she should always use a condom, but she says, "I had no idea how rampant a lot of STDs were or how easy they were to contract. I was really just trying to prevent HIV and pregnancy."

Don't be like Lydia. Learn from her mistakes and those of others who've been there. Educate yourself about the potential risks *before* the deed goes down, and be prepared to discuss them with your doctor and get tested for them. As we said before, even if you use condoms every time, they don't protect against all STDs.

We know it's not always the easiest topic to address, but it's also a good idea to quickly ask a guy if he's got anything you should know about—simple as that. Of course, he may not be honest, or he may not even know. According to the American Social Health Association (ASHA), an estimated fifteen

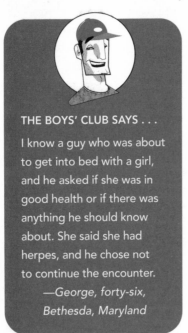

THE BOYS' CLUB SAYS . . .

I know a guy who was about to get into bed with a girl, and he asked if she was in good health or if there was anything he should know about. She said she had herpes, and he chose not to continue the encounter.

—George, forty-six,
Bethesda, Maryland

million people in the United States become infected with one or more STDs each year and an estimated sixty-five million people live with an incurable STD—but less than half of adults eighteen to forty-four years of age have ever been tested for an STD other than HIV/AIDS. So how would he know, and therefore how would you? Education, people! There are more than twenty-five diseases spread primarily by sexual activity, so it wouldn't hurt to read up on some of the biggies. If we haven't scared you enough yet, flip on over to appendix 2 for the lowdown on some of the telltale signs, symptoms, and more fun with STDs.

# No Time to Compromise

Even when you're aware of every last risk, when it comes to sex with someone you may not know all that well, beyond asking if they've got a disease, how do you bring up the topic of protection? Well, hopefully in this day and age, he's simply going to whip out a condom without you having to lead him down the path of enlightenment. Then again, there are a lot of weasels out there who still think that it's okay to have sex without slipping one on. Of course a lot of men may feel this way because: 1) they tend to lose some sensitivity when they wear one, and 2) the woman is the one who has to deal with an unwanted pregnancy if it comes to that, while he can just walk away without any real concerns or responsibilities.

Unfortunately, particularly if you don't know the guy all that well, he may not give two fucks about using protection—so you've simply got to be proactive and insist that he wear a condom. If he tries to convince you that it's not necessary, convince him that it is—as Stacy did with a certain bloke she picked up at a bar:

## SEXCAPADE: Open the Floodgates

*I was out with a friend one night, drinking up a storm, when this cute guy came up to us and said, "Sarah?!" to no one in particular. I'd certainly had scary guys try the slightly less subtle "Don't we know each other?" tactic before—but he was so adorable, I decided to pretend he'd got the name right. I said, "Yeah! Hey! How's it going?" just to see what he'd do next. He gave me this puzzled look, like he couldn't believe he'd really said the right name. Realizing I'd caught him off guard, and feeling kinder than usual that night, I apologized. "I'm sorry," I said. "My name's not really Sarah—it's Stacy." He laughed and looked kind of relieved. I said, "You didn't really think my name was Sarah, did you? You were just trying that to start a conversation." I guess that sounded like a good explanation to him, so he nodded and agreed.*

*At this point, my friend was a little annoyed that I was flirting with someone and had sort of bailed on her—but fortunately, when she went up to the bar to order a drink, a guy started hitting on her. So, I continued chatting with my new friend, who had an adorable English accent. I can't really remember what we talked about—all I know is that he had sort of a Jim Morrison look going on, with black leather pants and curly brown hair. Eventually we started making out, which got me tingling all over. I couldn't wait to have sex with this guy.*

*I turned to my friend, who looked somewhat irritated because she clearly didn't like the guy she was talking to. She came over and tried to talk to me and my Brit for a while. But pretty soon, he was out of control, rubbing up against me,* kissing me, and putting his tongue in my ear. My friend was trying to be understanding, but finally she said she was going to grab a cab and head home. I apologized to her, and she said she understood.

"So," I said to the guy. "What do you want to do now?" He could barely speak in complete sentences, he was so drunk, but he muttered something about sex and asked where I lived. Fortunately, my apartment was only a few blocks away. So, I suggested we head there. He eagerly agreed.

As we walked to my place, we stopped at practically every other storefront to make out. Finally, we got home, stripped, and collapsed on my living-room floor, where we kept going. After a while, he tried to go inside me without putting on a condom, so I stopped him. He tried begging, pleading, but I was sober enough at this point to tell him, "If you don't put one on, I'm not having sex with you, end of story." I went to my bedroom, grabbed one, and handed it to him. He grudgingly put it on.

As we were having sex, I felt his hand go down, and I thought maybe he was trying to take off the condom. Suddenly, I was really paranoid and asked him what he was doing. "Nuffing," he said, his accent becoming more grating than endearing at this point. Then, suddenly, there was this gush of liquid. I was absolutely convinced he'd slipped off the condom somehow and just come inside me.

"What happened?!" I demanded. He smiled sheepishly and said, "That was great." I asked him if he still had the condom on. Where was it? I wanted to know. Honestly, I can't even remember where it was, if it was on him or inside me. I was just flummoxed. In my crazed state, though, I decided he must have taken it off and I was going to get every disease known to sexually active womankind, as well as pregnant.

*The next morning, after getting the guy out of my place, I called Planned Parenthood and told them I'd had sex and the condom broke and I needed a morning-after pill. When I went in to get checked, I had an abnormal Pap as well (which fortunately turned out to be a false positive because of a yeast infection).*

*Within about a week, I had put the whole thing behind me, and with a little perspective, I realized something: I don't think the guy took the condom off at all. And I don't think it broke. Honestly? What I believe now is that I experienced what's known as female ejaculation—I think I came so hard that liquid just gushed out of me. Then again, I'm not completely sure. At least I didn't catch anything or get pregnant.*

*—Stacy, thirty-two, Seattle*

---

**SURVEY SAYS . . .**

According to the 2003 Durex Global Sex Survey, 26 percent of all Americans would have sex with a new partner who refused to wear a condom (scarier still was China—70 percent are horny enough to go for the love without the glove). According to our Happy Hook-Up survey, only 16 percent of male respondents have used a condom every time they've had casual sex. Yes, that means 84 percent of them jumped someone without a parachute at least once. And get this: 37 percent of them have had casual sex more than ten times without putting Mr. Happy in a helmet.

---

Not to make all men the bad guys here—a lot of them are perfectly willing to wear a condom, and many are as concerned about the spread of disease as you should be. But if they aren't, it's up to you to be proactive on every level—from asking him to wear one to having your own on hand to avoiding any action until that base is covered (along with his schlong). Whether the guy is concerned or not, you can always take matters into your own hands, just as Lucy did:

## SEXCAPADE: Phone It In

*Dave and I met on a blind date. I wasn't sure if there was going to be a real future for us, but I knew there was sexual chemistry, and I wanted to see where it would lead. After dinner and a few cocktails, we went back to my place to fool around. Things got hot and heavy pretty quick, and when we were ready to actually have intercourse, I opened my bedside table drawer and realized I had no condoms. I was praying he had one, but he shook his head and said he didn't. Fuck! (Or maybe not.)*

*I really wanted him and was so mad at myself for not having anything in the house. Then a lightbulb went off. I could just order them! I called a twenty-four-hour delivery service and asked them to bring over a pack, pronto. Twenty minutes later, my package had arrived—and then so did Dave's. Not only was the sex great—so was the mint chip ice cream I ordered for dessert.*

—Lucy, twenty-six, Washington, D.C.

# Condom Sense

You know you should always carry condoms with you or have them readily available in anticipation of a hook-up. "You ain't no ho just because you're prepared," notes former *Details* magazine and current *Razor* magazine sex columnist and author Anka Radakovich. But just to be on the safe-sex side, let's run through some common (and not so common) prophylactic practicalities:

## Rubber Research

It's awkward enough to ask him if he's got one, so get to know the condom aisle at your local drugstore and make sure you're well stocked. You should know the brand that works for you and always use it. You never know if you'll have some strange allergic reaction to the one he's been carrying in his wallet for the past ten months, and there is such a thing as being allergic to latex. On the allergy tip, you might want to keep latex *and* polyurethane varieties on hand (although studies show latex is your best bet for preventing pregnancy and STDs. *Never* go for lambskin, which can be porous). Also, keep them stashed in your bedside drawer for those times when you'll be entertaining at home. And be aware: There is an expiration date on condoms, so check them often and make sure you're not overdue for a new box; the shelf life of condoms, if stored correctly, is about three to five years.

## Don't Blow It

We know that sucking on a condom doesn't exactly sound fun for you or him, nor does using a dental dam for cunnilingus. That said, every expert we've talked to insists that using a barrier method for *absolutely every sex act*—including oral—is a nonnegotiable if you want to remain disease free. Our advice? Check out the wide assortment of flavored condoms and dental dams, often available at specialty sex shops, and consider making them a part of your casual sex foreplay. (However, some condoms are sold as novelty items only and don't protect you against disease or pregnancy, so make sure to check the package for any warnings.) You might actually impress your partner with your conscientious attention to disease prevention.

## Carrying Clue

Men don't have a lot of choices when it comes to hiding places; they generally need to carry condoms in their wallets. But here's a new option for the ladies: clean out an old compact. You'll find it's the perfect size to stash not just one but two condoms. Mark it with a piece of tape, so you'll know which one is for beauty and which is for bonking.

## No Glove, No Love

"If a guy refuses to wear a condom, say, 'If you won't cover your wang, we don't bang!'" advises Radakovich. If you're on the pill, use it only as backup since it doesn't protect against STDs.

## Handle with Care

The main reason condoms aren't guaranteed 100 percent effective at protecting against STDs and pregnancy is largely because they aren't used correctly. Study the instructions, which should come in every box, about how to put one on—and how to take it off afterwards—so you can help the poor guy out if he's not entirely skilled in that area. Also, don't handle them with sharp fingernails, and don't use them with an oil-based lubricant (which can damage the latex). You might even want to practice putting one on and taking it off on your own sometime (in the absence of a real penis, try using a vibrator or farm-fresh produce).

## Excuses, Excuses

We've all heard 'em—guys' tragic little excuses for riding bareback. So, make sure you've got a smart or sassy response and cut him off at the pass. Here's our top (or bottom) ten list of his pleas and your potential comebacks.

1. **Him:** "I'm too big."
   **You:** "That's too bad."

2. **Him:** "The condom's too big." (Seriously, lesser-endowed lovers have actually tried this one.)
   **You:** "Have fun with the little guy then . . . I've gotta go." (If he's too small, the condom may fall off—besides, is he really going to satisfy you with his itty bitty willy?)

3. **Him:** "It hurts."
   **You:** "Will blue balls feel better?"

4. **Him:** "They smell." (Yeah, yet he's all set to go butt-pirating.)
   **You:** "Planning on smelling your dick later? That I'd like to see."

5. **Him:** "I'm allergic to them."
   **You:** "The break out you get from an STD could be a lot worse."

6. **Him:** "But I lose fifty percent of the pleasure with it on."
   **You:** "You'll lose a hundred percent of the pleasure with it off."

7. **Him:** "I don't have any diseases."

   **You:** "Hey! Gross! What are those sores on your prick?!"

8. **Him:** "I don't need it—I'll pull out—I promise."

   **You:** "My pregnant friend Suzi heard that one seven months ago."

9. **Him:** "My ex never made me use one."

   **You:** "Your ex is an idiot—but I'll be happy to get her on the phone for you."

10. **Him:** "I don't know how to put it on."

    **You:** "I can't believe I'm saying this, but let me show you."

In sum, although we should hardly have to tell you this, casual sex is far from an appropriate time to play Russian roulette—let alone start an accidental family. If you want to have a backup plan to protect yourself against pregnancy, such as using the pill, that's certainly not a bad idea—but you still need to be condom-conscious and proactive with prophylactics at all times. Whether you have casual sex only once in your life or it's a regular practice, simply learn to make the good old barrier method your very best friend. Ultimately, you'll be a whole lot happier and healthier.

*Getting Your Body*

*Ready for Action*

# Chapter Three

# The Bedding Planner

On a lighter note, there are certain aspects of getting ready for casual sex that have nothing to do with pregnancy, infections, diseases, or death (aren't you glad we got that out of the way, though?). Yes, we're talking about how you look and feel (maybe for him, but, more important, for *yourself* and your own self-confidence in the sack). Don't worry—you don't have to be a supermodel to get some action. Sure, 68 percent of the men who participated in our Happy Hook-Up survey ranked being "attractive" as the first quality they look for in a casual sex contender (the other 32 percent ranked "sexual skill" as the top quality; so much for the "smart" and "sensitive" girls!), but they also noted that there are plenty of ways to attract them (surprise, surprise). If you simply pay attention to the basic, commonsense personal-care practices, then add in a little sass and self-confidence, chances are you'll be golden. Let's delve a bit deeper into those details.

# Lookin' Good

From hair, makeup, and attire to personal hygiene, diet, and exercise, it's always good to take care of yourself and feel sexy in your own skin, whether you plan on getting laid or not. Our experts offer these key ingredients—some obvious, some that may not be so readily apparent—for making yourself aesthetically equipped for anything.

## Beauty Tips for Sexual Bliss

1. **Trim the Hedges, Clean the House.** Few things are worse than that not-so-fresh feeling—and chances are it's going to get in the way of enjoying the deed every time. So bathe on a regular basis (we didn't need to tell you that, did we?). Don't douche—it's unnecessary if you cleanse yourself regularly and, according to the National Institutes of Health, it removes some of the normal protective bacteria in the vagina and increases the risk of getting some sexually transmitted diseases. Shave or remove hair regularly—legs, armpits, bikini line. (How much hair you remove is really up to you, though; in a 2003 survey conducted by Oxygen TV's *Talk Sex*, 40 percent of men prefer that their partner be shaved clean, 46 percent prefer the pubic hair to be trimmed, and 14 percent like it au naturel.) A Q-tip or cotton ball with a few drops of Visine can help eliminate any post–hair removal irritations or bumps. And don't forget the deodorant under your arms and a spritz of unoffending fragrance on your pulse points.

2. **Go Natural.** When it comes to your hair and makeup and casual sex, less is more. That is, the less you have to remove before or during the deed, the better. Essentially, apply the amount that makes you feel like your fine self, but not so

much that it's going to get all over him and the sheets and smear around your face.

3. Take It with You. For those times when you may be doing the morning-after breakfast, you'll want to be able to do a little touch-up, so you don't look like that girl you saw last Sunday morning at the café with the mascara smudges under her bleary eyes. Your kit should include eyedrops, perfume, lip balm, breath mints or gum, and select cosmetics you can't do without. Of course, beauty is only skin-deep. That said, disregard our advice and you could find yourself in a situation like Carrie:

## SEXCAPADE:
## There's Something about Carrie

*I hate dancing, but somehow my friends convinced me to join them for a night out on the town one weekend. We wound up drinking so much and had such a good time, we closed the place down. Out in front, we were trying to figure out where we could go to keep partying when this adorable guy walked by us with his dogs. He stopped long enough for us to pet the dogs, and my friend started talking to him, asking him if he knew of anywhere we could go to get a beer. He said we could go to his place—he lived just up the road. So, oblivious to the fact that our new acquaintance could be a serial killer, we decided to take him up on the offer (my other friend was a big guy, so it wasn't totally risky).*

*My girlfriend and I hung back while our guy friend and the hot guy chatted up ahead of us. My friend turned to me and said, "I think he's an actor!" We could barely make out* what the guys were saying up ahead, but then we heard the name of a cheesy local band. I won't say who it was, though I will say this guy was both an actor and a drummer. We climbed higher up into the hills, and soon we were at this beautiful house with a panoramic view of Hollywood.

My friend and I raided hot guy's fridge and found some wine. After a bunch of flirting between me and hot guy and a tragic jam session with all four of us in the rehearsal space below his garage, my friend suggested we start a massage line (gotta love that girl). I was in front with hot guy right behind me. After a few minutes, he asked how I was doing and if I needed to lie down. Feeling even bolder than usual, I took my cue, turned to my friends, and said, "[Hot guy] and I are going into his room to have sex now." My friends looked at each other, laughed, and said, "Okay." Hot guy told them to have fun, feel free to use the Jacuzzi downstairs, and crash in the guest room.

Then, we were off to his room. We had such hot sex, he actually said to me in the middle, "Can we do this again?"— and we hadn't even finished the first round! I really wanted to stick around for more. But, when I excused myself to go to the bathroom and checked myself out in the mirror, I was a mess. I went to find my purse and realized that I'd left all my makeup in my car, which was way down the hill, back at the bar. I rummaged through hot guy's bathroom drawers and cabinets, but couldn't find anything that would conceal the blotchy spots on my skin or improve my appearance even slightly.

So, at around 4 A.M., I told hot guy I was going to take off. On top of looking like crap, I felt a splitting headache coming on. He looked surprised that I wanted to leave and practically begged for one more time. So, we had a final send-off session, which I must admit was amazing. (I'm just glad it was still dark

*and he couldn't really see whom he was doing.) Afterwards,*
*I gave him a kiss good-bye—quickly ran downstairs to let my*
*friends know I was leaving (they were too tired to get up and*
*leave with me)—and made my exit just as the sun was coming*
*up.*

*I was a little mortified as a couple of early risers jogged*
*by me. I tried to keep my head down as they yelled a cheery*
*"Good morning!" The worst part? When I got in my car—talk*
*about a* There's Something about Mary *moment—I looked in*
*the rearview mirror to see a huge glob of the guy's splooge just*
*starting to stiffen in my hair and on my forehead.*

—Carrie, thirty-four, Hollywood

# Fashion 411

They say that clothes make the man, but in the case of casual sex, they can also make the woman—and your night. While your attire is always going to be a matter of personal preference, and chances are you'll know what works for you, there are also certain styles that will be better for hooking up than others. No, we're not talking about fishnets or splooge-proof vinyl. The ways you can dress to impress on your way to casual sex are, once again, mostly a matter of basic common sense.

## Style Tips for Sexual Bliss

1. Keep It Simple. If you're going to be out all night, and perhaps even doing a little morning-after strut-of-satisfaction and/or breakfast, the last thing you want to be wearing is uncomfortable, flashy, complicated clothing. Go with classic styles that can translate to any time of day, whenever possible. "Demure is

always better," says *Shape* magazine style director Jacqui Stafford. "Don't wear anything so low cut that you come across as desperate." Then again, if it's been a while and you want everyone to know you got action, wear something crazy and sassy and, by all means, flaunt what you've got the next morning as you hold your head up high.

2. Opt for Easy Access. No, you don't need to wear crotchless panties and a miniskirt, but you might want to don something that doesn't require more than a few minutes to take off (and get back on). You never know how quickly you'll want to tear off that hot little number—or how speedily you'll want to replace it to make a quick getaway. "Never wear underthings that are difficult for a man to get off," adds Stafford. "They get confused easily, and fumbling is unsexy."

3. Power Dress. Simple and classic doesn't have to equal conservative. You should select a style that flatters your figure and gives you a burst of confidence. "Always wear something you know you look drop-dead gorgeous in," says Stafford. Perhaps you have a lucky outfit that draws the men to you or a piece of jewelry that puts you in a sassy mind-set. Whatever it is, wear it with pride—and don't forget to pay as much attention to what they might see later as what they see straight off the bat. Wear a matching bra and panties in your favorite color and style for optimum self-assurance all the way down to the base layer. (Dr. Ava agrees, suggesting you not only wear your "sexiest lingerie"—but let your partner know about it, so he's aware of what he can expect later.)

## Fashion Dos and Don'ts

There are, of course, certain rules you can follow to keep your attire simple and classy. Stafford adds the following advice:

- Do wear a great coat to hide your outfit underneath, so you don't look like a working girl.

- Don't wear something you've just bought that day in the sale unless you know you look fabulous.

- Do wear fabulous underthings or nothing at all.

- Don't wear underthings that need a good wash or look like they're past their prime.

- Do wear high, strappy shoes—the higher and strappier, the better. (Even if there's a snowstorm. Men don't care about snowstorms.)

- Don't forget the pedicure. Imperative.

---

**SEXPRESSIONS**

**cleaverage,** *n.*, tactic used by a woman to seduce a man in which she wears a low-cut top. Her cleavage allows her a certain amount of leverage with said conquest, allowing her to get what she wants.

e.g., "Sandra used her cleaverage to get the bartender into bed."

## Fashion 911

There will obviously be times when you're not planning on having a one-night stand—sometimes it just happens, and you may find yourself unprepared. In that situation, you should not only assess whether or not you have the requisite protection, but do a quick beauty and fashion check, and figure out if it's really going to be worth your while or a waste of time. Maybe you look okay to him, but are you clothed and groomed for optimum action? For instance:

How hard is it going to be to undress and redress? Do your legs feel as smooth as silk or like an Arizona cactus? There are a lot of things to consider—things our friend Emma might have been well served in assessing:

## SEXCAPADE:
## These Boots Weren't Made for Bonking

*There was this new techno club in town where I met up with my friends for a few drinks. As we headed out on the dance floor, I kept checking out this one guy who had these cool-looking glasses on that kind of reminded me of Bono during "The Fly" era. As the hours passed, the club was starting to clear out, but my friends and I were still out dancing—and so was "Bono."*

*As it turns out, he was friends with a couple of people in the group I was at the club with, and when the place closed, he asked if he could get a ride with us. He was flirting with me a little on the way to the car, and after I dropped off all of my friends at their cars, he was the only one left. I asked him where his car was, and he slyly said, "At my place." I looked at him with a bit of skepticism, as I'd hooked up with enough guys recently to know this game, and I wasn't really out to get laid that night.*

*"Alright, then I guess I'll have to drive you home," I said.*

*"Yeah, if you don't mind," he said— a little too enthusiastically.*

*"Just so you know, though, I'm really not interested in having sex with you," I said as firmly as I could.*

"Okay, thanks for the warning," he shot back quickly, trying to stifle a laugh.

"Seriously," I said. "I've had enough of you guys lately."

"What guys would those be?" asked Bono.

"The ones who think they can sleep with anyone they want, just because they're kind of cute," I replied.

"Oh, okay," he said, still smirking. "Rejection's bad enough, but being called 'cute' really kills the ego even more."

When we pulled up at Bono's house, I could already feel myself starting to cave a little bit. I mean, I'd been so obnoxious, assuming this guy wanted to sleep with me, and the way he was laughing at me was actually kind of appealing.

"Alright, well, this is it," he said. "So, I guess you should probably go now—since you don't want to have sex with me."

I couldn't help laughing. "Man, you're just so cute, aren't you?" I said—emphasizing the word cute as much as possible.

"Yeah, but that won't get me any action, apparently," he laughed. After a mildly awkward pause, he said, "But would it get me a kiss . . . ?"

How could I resist? I leaned toward him. About ten minutes later, we were still making out in my car. Finally, we stopped.

"Sure you don't want to come in?" Bono asked. "I have a pretty cool setup in there."

"What kind of setup are you referring to?" I asked.

"I do laser light shows for a living," he said. "I'd love to show you this new project I'm working on—it's pretty rockin'."

"And maybe after that I can take a look at your etchings?" I joked.

He looked at me like he didn't get it—in fact, I could tell he didn't. Okay, so he wasn't all that bright, but there was something there.

Cut to ten minutes later, on his couch, watching some cheesy light show on a giant screen in his living room. We started making out again, and pretty soon, he started trying to put his hand down my skirt. I'd already figured I was going to give in, so I let him keep going.

That's when I realized—things might get complicated. It was the middle of winter, so I had these thick tights on under my skirt and, worse still, knee-high boots that laced all the way up. How the hell was I going to get undressed, so we could have sex?

Bono looked down, trying to figure out how he was going to get my clothes off. I looked down too, embarrassed.

"I guess we're not going to have sex after all," I said. "This outfit's going to take an hour to get off."

"Damn," said Bono, clearly disappointed. "Well, why don't you come into the bedroom—we can just hang out a little longer."

I agreed. After making out for another half hour on his bed, I really was ready to explode, and I could tell he was too. So, I decided we could just do it with our clothes on.

"I have an idea . . ." I said, lifting up my skirt, and tugging down my tights and underwear as far as my knees, where the boots prevented them from going any further.

"Cool," muttered Bono, yanking down his pants and wriggling to get under me. He grabbed a condom and we were off.

Unfortunately, all I could think about was how trampy I felt. And on top of that, the sex wasn't even very good. I guess we'd been making out for so long that he was already on the way to climax . . . so after about three or four minutes, he was done.

*"Okay then," I said. "That was great . . . thanks . . . I should probably be going now."*

*"Oh, alright," said Bono. "Well, let me at least walk you out."*

*"Sure," I said, pulling my tights up and smoothing my skirt down over them. At least I could make a quick getaway, and that was all I wanted to do after that experience.*

*As I was walking out, Bono asked if he could get my number.*

*"Why?" I asked. "It's not like we'll ever see each other again."*

*"Oh," he said. "Um, well, can I give you my number—you know, just in case?"*

*"Alright," I agreed. "But don't expect me to call."*

*Then, Bono handed me his card, which read, LEO'S LASER LIGHT SHOWS. GET ROCKED!!! Scary. I still have the card as a souvenir. Not only does it make me laugh every time I see it—it also serves as a constant reminder to never wear my knee-high, lace-up boots out to a club, whether I plan on getting laid or not.*

—Emma, thirty-nine, Brooklyn

Obviously, Emma felt good—and was looking good—but she realized a little too late in the game that she wasn't properly dressed for the casual deed. On the other hand, there are times when your attire will give you incredible confidence, not to mention more action options than you ever thought possible. In those instances, assuming all other factors are fornication friendly, why not just go for it? That's what Charli decided after captivating a young lover with one particular piece of clothing:

## Sexcapade: The Magic Bustier

*One Saturday night at a costume party down on the Peninsula, I was ready to go home when the deejay made his way across the lawn and said he really wanted to kiss me.*

*"Why don't you then? Never be afraid to ask for what you want," I said, feeling like a wise older woman. I stood on tip-toe, and he gave me a nice, long kiss. I liked his lips and how tall he was. After spooning by the sound-mixing table, we snuck around the side of the house, where other couples were making out. There were also plenty of guys relieving themselves in the general vicinity, but we didn't care. I definitely preferred this deejay to the less attractive guy I'd made out with while bump-and-grinding across the dance floor earlier.*

*What amazed me, though, was that I—a forty-four-year-old woman—had spent the evening kissing not just one but two men (boys actually). I'm sure they were both about half my age. I was even a little surprised that both guys had zeroed in on me, despite the fact that there were plenty of hot little hula girls in their twenties dancing around. Maybe it was my black-framed glasses, the character etched on my face, or the fact that I seemed low maintenance and fun, with no expectations— but I figured it probably had more to do with my bustier. I'm not exactly stacked—I've got no boobs to boost—but the two times I've worn that top, I've been swarmed by male admirers.*

*I'd found the bustier in a thrift store four years before and decided it was perfect for my Venus flytrap Halloween costume. The first night I wore it, I scored a great big pirate with* long curly black hair and, after a swashbuckling night on the high seas of my futon bed, I never saw him again. I wondered briefly if he was disappointed when the bustier came off, but since I was sleeping with more than one guy at the time, I didn't really care.

As my deejay manned his mixing board, we chatted about art and music and travel—between lip locks. He lived in Montana but spun for parties all over the West. Since he had to stay to the end of the party, I gave him my phone number and drove back to San Francisco with friends.

When I woke up, I already had two messages, one inviting me to breakfast on the beach, which I was sad to have missed. At noon, he called again and said he'd like to meet after he repaired his blown amplifier. He called me hourly to make sure I was still interested—and at one point, I wasn't certain I was. After all, in this day and age, what was a middle-aged woman doing planning an afternoon tryst?

But soon after he showed up at my house, my deejay was tasting every last part of my body, unfazed by the change in my silhouette, now that my bustier was gone. "How is it possible that such a beautiful woman is single?" he asked, unaware of San Francisco dynamics. "I can't believe my luck," he mumbled as he nibbled me to nirvana. That night I reluctantly sent him to the airport for his next gig in Seattle.

Afterwards, I started reflecting and realized: I'd sure like to find a guy with a little stick-to-it-ness—but if I ever want a little no-strings-attached sex, all I have to do is find myself a costume party and zip myself into my magic bustier.

—Charli, forty-six, San Francisco

# Foxy Ladies

Whether it's a lucky top, a certain accessory, the way you wear your hair or don a pair of old blue jeans, women around the country have their own secret-weapon styles for scoring a guy. Here's what some of them told us about their get-lucky looks:

- *"I've got a push-up bra that always seems to drive guys wild. Sometimes I wonder if it's just that I feel like my tits look amazing when I wear it—whatever it is, I swear the men flock to me every time."* —Vivian, twenty-three, Charleston, South Carolina

- *"A tight black dress is all it takes to draw some guy's attention to me—and if I like the look of him, I'll be getting lucky that night. It's also incredibly easy to get on and off . . . after I get off."* —Grace, forty, Miami

- *"Every time I wear my hair in braids, along with a halter top and jeans, I get a lot of attention—and it usually leads to action."* —Audra, twenty-six, Woodland Hills, California

- *"I wear any kind of hat and high-heeled shoes. Works every time."* —Cameron, thirty-nine, Falmouth, Massachusetts

- *"I like to put on a funky piece of old jewelry whenever I go out. It might be a pair of big earrings, an unusual ring or necklace. It's all about wearing something eye-catching. If a guy digs it, he'll come over and immediately have something to compliment me on, which usually leads to lots of flirting and possible fucking."* —Sonja, twenty-eight, Seattle

- *"I just show lots of skin. Some people might think it's slutty, but who cares? If a cute guy thinks it's slutty enough in a good way, he's mine for the night."* —Janice, twenty-one, Philadelphia

- *"I just wear a baseball hat. Yup, guys love a girl who has the guts to go to a bar wearing a baseball hat. It works for me every time. It's also an icebreaker. For example, if I wear a hat with NY on it, guys come up to me and say 'Oh, are you a New York Yankees fan?' It sort of takes the edge off of the next question: 'Can I buy you a drink?' The hat, coupled with a tight white T-shirt...it's a sure thing."* —Kiki, thirty-two, Santa Monica, California

# Feelin' Good

While your beauty regime and fashion sense are certainly important aspects of getting yourself ready for action, there are deeper issues to address as well. That is, you need to be your best inside and out. Everyone knows that when you feel good, it shows. You glow and radiate a bit of animal attraction because you're completely comfortable in your own skin. To achieve this and ensure your ultimate satisfaction—as well as preventing any unfortunate little accidents along the way—we suggest the following.

## Body Tips for Sexual Bliss

1. **Don't Masturbate.** Well, go ahead if you're about to burst. But, just as guys are advised to squeeze one off before doing the deed with a partner (so they can last longer during intercourse)—women may already be spent and have a harder time achieving orgasm if they've already serviced themselves. And isn't the whole idea to get off? (It should be. Try it, you'll like it.)

2. **Go Easy on the Fiber.** We can tell you that it pays to know your trigger foods—whether you're going to get lucky or not. It may be as obvious as avoiding a bean burrito, or maybe pasta or dairy products always leave you feeling bloated and

gassy. Whatever it is for you, avoid 'em unless you're sure you'll be spending an evening alone. Laxatives are a big no-no as well, since they're guaranteed to give you the runs.

3. Work Out. Not only does exercise make you feel good about yourself and your body, it's actually been shown to increase your sexual appetite, which can only be a good thing, right? In addition to getting a few strength and cardio workouts a week, there are certain exercises you can do to keep your love muscles (aka pubococcygeus, or "PC," muscles) in top condition, which is known to increase the intensity of your orgasms (hurray!). These exercises are known as kegels; all you have to do to keep your vaginal muscles tight and toned is to contract them as often as possible (think about what you do when you're trying to keep yourself from peeing, or try stopping yourself from peeing mid-flow to master it—simple as that).

### Double Your Pleasure

If you're not sure how to do kegel exercises correctly, kinky advice on the topic abounds. For instance, women's health experts suggest that you lie down, put your finger inside your vagina, and then attempt to squeeze, as if you were trying to stop yourself from urinating. If you feel tightness on your finger, you're squeezing the right pelvic muscle. Naturally, you may not want to stop there—once you've got your finger in and the clenching begins, why not just finish yourself off? Just make sure it's not right before you go out—remember? We said no masturbating prior to a hook-up.

## Sexercise! The Pre-Whoopie Workout

Exercise doesn't have to suck. If you're heading out for a night on the town and aren't feeling your firmest, slimmest, sexiest self, try this quick, five-minute strength workout designed by renowned fitness expert Linda Shelton to give your body a speedy semi-sculpt.

1. Alternating lunges. Stand erect, feet hip-width apart; then take a large step forward with right foot. Lower hips as you bend right knee to ninety degrees, aligning right knee with right ankle as left knee points toward floor, heel lifted. Push off right foot to return to standing position, then repeat with left foot. Alternate lunges for twelve to fifteen reps on each side. *Strengthens buttocks, hamstrings, and quadriceps*

2. Push-ups. Kneel on all fours with arms straight, hands in line with shoulders. Extend legs, so you're supported on hands and balls of feet, or keep knees on floor. Contract abs, so body forms one straight line from head to heels (or hips). Bend elbows to lower chest toward floor, until elbows are even with shoulders. Push up to return to starting position and repeat for twelve to fifteen reps. *Strengthens chest, front shoulders, and triceps*

3. Tri-dips. Sit on the edge of a chair, knees bent and aligned with ankles, feet flat. Place your hands on the seat, shoulder-width apart, arms straight and fingers facing forward. Contract your abs, press down with your hands, and lift your butt off the seat, so you're supported by your arms. Draw shoulder blades down and together. Maintain an erect torso as you bend your arms, lowering hips toward floor until elbows align with shoulders. Press back up to return to starting position and repeat for twelve to fifteen reps. *Strengthens triceps*

4. **Bridge lifts.** Lie on back, arms flat on floor at your sides, palms down, knees bent with feet flat on floor and aligned with knees. Use your butt and hamstring muscles to lift your hips until your body forms one straight line from shoulders to knees. Lower torso back to floor and repeat for twelve to fifteen reps. *Strengthens buttocks, hamstrings, and spine extensors (back)*

5. **Crunches.** Lie on your back, knees bent and feet flat on floor, hands behind head with fingers unclasped. Contract your abs, bringing lower ribs and hips toward each other; then slowly lift your upper torso until shoulder blades are off the floor. Lower and repeat for twelve to fifteen reps. *Strengthens abdominals*

## A Few More Notes on Flatulence

When it comes to the one-night stand, there are booty calls, and then there are *booty calls* of a different kind. It's embarrassing enough when you let a little something escape from your buttocks around someone you know deeply, intimately—so just imagine the horror of being visited by the flatulent fairy in the company of a guy with whom you're just getting busy (or with whom you just got busy). Sure it happens to everyone, and it shouldn't be a huge deal. By the same token, when it does transpire in the midst of a fleeting tryst, it can make for a bit of an awkward situation—even if you're the only one who hears it. Sometimes there's nothing you can do about it, but our advice on being conscious of your trigger foods could save you from disgrace, as our friend Casey can confirm:

## SEXCAPADE: Bartender Blowout

*I used to go to this Indian restaurant all the time, where the curry was hot and the waiters were hotter. One night, while there with some friends, after several large beers and some of the best curry I've ever had, I got up the nerve to go over to the bartender and start up a conversation. When my friends came over to say they were headed to another club, I told him where we were going and asked him to meet up with us later.*

*About an hour later, I was thrilled when I saw the restaurant bartender walk into the club. He came right over to me, and we started dancing—incredibly close. He was rubbing up against me, and it was getting me so hot. I told my friends that I thought I was going to take off with him, and they told me to have fun.*

*He drove us back to my place, where we had amazing sex and I fell asleep in his arms. It must have been a few hours later when this incredibly loud noise woke me up. Turns out, it was me—I'd just let out one of the loudest farts I've ever released in my life. I was mortified, but I just tried to pretend I was tossing and turning in a new position, and prayed he hadn't heard. I think I even tried to rub my foot along the sheets to achieve the same sort of sound, but nothing could really mask or mimic what I'd just done.*

*The next morning, my bartender didn't let on that he'd heard anything ... but, much to my dismay, he also left politely—*

*didn't ask for my number or say he wanted to see me again. To this day, I'm convinced it's because he heard me fart. And I'll tell you, I've never been back to that Indian restaurant again. In fact, I try to avoid curry, particularly combined with beer, at all costs, especially if I know I'm going to be out, and there's any chance of getting any action.*

—Casey, thirty-eight, Boston

---

---

**queef,** *n., v.,* more commonly known as the "pussy fart," or the act of releasing said fart, this little noise generally doesn't smell, but can be incredibly embarrassing. It's usually caused by your partner creating air pockets in your vagina, either with his fingers, tongue, or penis.

e.g., "Right in the middle of having sex with Paul, Marilyn queefed—but managed to avert embarrassment, for the most part, by exclaiming, 'Dude, that was *so your fault!*'"

# Bein' Good

Finally, when preparing for your casual encounter, you need to make sure that you act appropriately—that you take the necessary precautions beyond protection, appearance, and bodily functions. We're talking about having your wits about you and ensuring that, in the event that anything should go wrong, you won't find yourself in a dangerous or undesirable situation from which you may not be able to escape. Therefore, based on the advice of a number of experts, we urge you to consider the following.

## Behavioral Tips for Sexual Bliss

1.  **Get a Friend's Approval.** Your friends can play a very important part in the safe casual sex experience. They should be your barometer, and you should be theirs. It's not always possible to have a friend screen a potential hook-up, but when it is, take the time to introduce your conquest to your cohort(s) so you can get a second opinion (or more). Your mantra? *Friends don't let friends do jerks.*

2.  **Share the Details.** If you receive the thumbs-up on your hook-up, be smart and let your friend(s) know where you're planning on going, and plan a check-in time—either they call you or you call them. In a world filled with cell phones and two-way pagers, this rule is so easy to follow. "Always let someone know where you're going, always have a cell phone with you, and always take your own car," agrees Dr. Ava. If you're particularly cautious (we know, you probably wouldn't be going for it)—leave the details of where you'll be on a friend's answering machine, so they'll be absolutely clear on where the hell you are when they stumble home at three in the morning.

3.  **Take a Sobriety Test.** You should especially make sure to get a friend's go-ahead if you've been consuming alcohol (just make sure your pal is reasonably sober—there's nothing like two drunk girls thinking Mr. Scary is seriously sexy). If you're not sure you're okay to get behind the wheel, for instance, you're definitely not okay to take a ride on the man of the hour. Jenny can tell you as much:

## SEXCAPADE: **Down the Hatch**

*I once woke up naked in some guy's bed whose name I couldn't remember—in fact, I couldn't even pick him out of a lineup if I needed to. I had to call my girlfriend I'd gone out with the night before to tell her I didn't know where I was and how hung over I was. She suggested I get in a cab ASAP and get to her house. I got dressed as quietly as possible, trying not to wake this guy up, and stumbled out of the apartment. I had to go to a pay phone outside because I didn't want to have to ask him where I was. I gave the taxi the cross streets and couldn't wait to get to my friend's place. All I could do was hope to never bump into the guy again. The worst/funniest part about it is that I wouldn't even know if I had or not, since I have no idea what he looked like.*

—Jenny, thirty-six, Chapel Hill, North Carolina

As we've said, because casual sex is often a spur-of-the-moment thing, you're obviously not going to be able to plan every last detail—aesthetic or otherwise—before the deed goes down. However, we like to think the mere possibility that you might meet a guy for a bit of commitment-free fun is a great excuse to take care of yourself. From diet and exercise to personal hygiene to beauty-and-style practices to safety precautions, if you tend to all this business, you're simply going to kick your overall well-being into overdrive, and that's whether you get laid or not. So when you get right down to it, being a bedding planner makes for a better you—as ridiculously cheesy as it sounds, as Milli Vanilli said, "Girl, you know it's true."

## Alcohol & Action: Notes to Self

Going straight for a little casual sex when you're inebri-
ated, or otherwise out of your head, is often a given.
In fact, according to our Happy Hook-Up survey, 30
percent of women have *never* been sober when having
casual sex (in truth, that's 24 percent, since 6 percent
of respondents have never had casual sex at all, though).
That's why there are damn good reasons to stay sober—
or at least moderately so. While a good buzz can be
fine for decreasing inhibitions and getting you all hot
and bothered, consider the flip side of that coin:

**Coyote Ugly.** He seemed so incredibly hot after that
fifth Long Island iced tea! But, after the fun, he turns
back into the elephant man. Oops.

**Dehydrated and Hung Over.** There's dry humping,
and then there's being a dry hump. No fun for anyone—
particularly when combined with a splitting headache.
Drinking a glass of water between cocktails is never a
bad idea, especially when it comes to sex. You need to
be well lubricated, and the more alcohol you drink, the
more dehydrated you'll be.

**Danger, Will Robinson!** To be smart, careful, safe,
and, most important, cautious, about picking a sex
partner, you need to be reasonably sober. Too many
cocktails and you wind up throwing caution to the wind—
which can be incredibly risky business. Suddenly, you
forget to use condoms, or anal sex sounds like a great
idea, or, well, you're doing any number of things you
never would have considered in a sober state.

*Where to Find 'Em—*

*And the Ups and Downs*

*(and Ups and Downs)*

*of Each Prospect*

# Chapter Four

# The Meet Market

now—finally—you should be good and ready for just about any casual sex that might come your way. You've got your head screwed on straight, protection close at hand, and you're looking and feeling like your sassiest, most fabulous self. All that's left to do is find the guy who will get you going—simple enough, right?

Okay, maybe you don't think so, but it's really not that tough. In fact, your options for action are pretty much limitless. Every time you walk out the door, you're bound to encounter a man or two who might be worth your while. Of course, as always, think the situation through clearly; you should particularly consider the context in which you encounter each prospect.

Some questions to ask yourself: How and where are you crossing paths with the guy—and do you come here often? (It's not a cheesy line when you're asking it of yourself.) In other words, is this someone you're running into randomly, or are you going to bump into him again and again (meaning you'll get to be reminded of what happened between you—good or bad—every time you do)? How well do you know this person—perhaps a little too well? If you *are* going to have to see him repeatedly after the fact, how are you going to feel about that—and how might he deal with it?

Oh, and we're just getting started here. Let's put it another way—or actually, we'll let Ruth, twenty-three, of Los Angeles, illustrate: "If you have sex with your friends, you're fucked. If you have sex with your neighbors, you are also fucked. If you have sex with your friend who happens to be your neighbor, then it's time to move."

Of course, things don't have to be that grim—you simply need to weigh the pros and cons of the situation at hand. The great thing is that there are so many people with whom a prime opportunity for casual sex can arise—not to mention ideal locations to find them. So, let's run through some of the likely suspects and scenarios that might provide these prospects and determine the ups and downs: what could possibly go right—or horribly wrong.

# People Who Need People

In this world of Friendsters and MySpacers, circles of acquaintances and limitless networking opportunities, the people you know are a great way to access casual sex options. That is, you're not always going to be hooking up with complete strangers; you may have encountered them often, or infrequently. Perhaps you've considered them for a little casual coitus; perhaps you haven't. The real question is, should you or shouldn't you? Yes, you're getting used to this—here's the part where we break it down for you.

## Friendly Fornication

As Ruth so eloquently suggested, when you fuck your friends, you also run the risk of fucking the friendship. Of course, she later told us, "My best casual sex was with my best friend. He ended up having a ten-inch cock, so it was awesome." Hence, the gray areas abound in this scenario. As Linda, thirty-two, of Los Angeles, says, "Certain friends can be good—the ones you know you can throw back a couple cocktails with, be sheepish about it in the morning with, but not let it ruin your friendship. Otherwise, stick to total strangers." The sex might also be excellent because you feel so comfortable with each other and can

**THE BOYS' CLUB SAYS . . .**

Don't fuck your friends: that falls into shitting where you eat. If you have to fuck your friend, go jerk off somewhere.

—Chuck, thirty-four, Cleveland

turn to each other as advisors or make the sex an extension of your friendship—as Theresa, thirty-seven, of Hollywood, discusses in a few pages.

Then again, you need to consider if there's a reason you think of this person as a friend and not a boyfriend. (If it's a girlfriend you're considering hooking up with, see "Lesbo Lust" later in the chapter—although the song may remain the same.) If you're "just friends," chances are you have a lot in common, but sexual chemistry isn't on that list. If it *is*—well then, guess what? You might just have yourself a real bona fide boyfriend-girlfriend relationship, not a casual sexual one and not a platonic one. As Marsha, thirty-five, of Saratoga, New York, says, "If I have sex with a friend I already like and enjoy spending time with, and now we're enjoying each other sexually too, we've moved past the friendship stage."

There's also the possibility that the two of you haven't slept together because only one of you has those "not just like them but *like them like them*" feelings. If that's the case, the person with those special feelings is clearly screwed (but not literally). Sometimes, even though all the signs don't point to go, you may decide you want to test the waters to see how far you can take it; that generally screws things up as well. "I've slept with quite a few guy friends, and it was definitely weird afterwards," agrees Sarah, thirty-five, of San Francisco. "It basically ruined my friendship with one of my best guy friends in college. In retrospect, he was kind of an ass and therefore not worth getting upset about, but at the time, it was very emotionally difficult. I'm not saying the relationship won't be able to survive a casual sex encounter, but it's almost guaranteed to change your friendship—at least for a while."

Bottom line: You've got five options.

1. Remain friends and keep your hands off of each other's nether regions.

2. Sleep together and destroy the relationship.

3. Sleep together and become the oh-so-rare/nearly extinct but successful "friends who fuck."

4. Have a real committed and monogamous relationship (if you're equally and reciprocally into everything about each other).

5. If one of you is pining for the other, that person needs to get over the unrequited love crap, get a life, and find someone who's interested. And that's what friends are supposed to be for. Help each other out, would you?

| Ups | Downs |
| --- | --- |
| A true friend is forever. | You could lose a true friend forever. |
| Knowing each other so well can equal less awkwardness. | Things can get pretty awkward when the clothes come off. |
| This could take your relationship to an entirely new level. | That level could be the basement . . . next stop: hell. |

## A Friend in Need Is a Friend Indeed

*The year I moved out of my crappy little single into a great apartment, I was having a blast, meeting a lot of really cute boys, and feeling good about living in Los Angeles after years of suburban boredom. Hollywood guys were sexy, mysterious, and cool, and I wanted nothing more than to rock their worlds. There was just one problem, in my mind: I was a twenty-two-year-old who'd had about four lovers in her entire life, and I wanted to be amazing in bed, including being able to give the perfect blow job—and while I had done it before, I wasn't sure I knew what I was doing.*

*So, I decided to turn to Jimmy—one of my first crushes—for a little friendly advice. We'd slept together on occasion, but there was a very delicate balance we were able to strike between attraction, respect, and possibility. I think we just sort of mutually and silently decided that we could be friends who fuck, but we weren't the right fit as boyfriend and girlfriend.*

*On this one particular night, a little bored, I called Jimmy. After a while—and I honestly cannot remember how the topic came up—we were talking about oral sex. After a few exchanges, I asked him what he was up to that night. He didn't have plans, and so I just said, "How's about coming over here and teaching me how to give head?" First: silence, quickly followed by, "Okay."*

*In retrospect, it was pretty mechanical: he knocked; I answered the door. He entered my bedroom and made himself comfortable in the center of my beat-up futon. I was nervous but, like any good student, was willing and, more important, had the desire to succeed. I won't go into the particulars of his instruction, but suffice to say it involved things that hadn't really dawned on me before: rhythm, hand movements, tongue, and most important, letting the recipient know that you are enjoying yourself and you want to be doing it. I would liken my pre-Jimmy blow jobs to quickly melting a Popsicle in my mouth. I had no concept of technique. I thought the guy was lucky just being in my mouth. Jimmy changed all that. I was educated and grateful—and after that, the guys I was with were grateful too!*

*Several weeks later, I started seeing someone who, after our first night together, paid me the biggest compliment a late bloomer like me could have hoped for: he told me how much he liked our chemistry in bed, that he hadn't fucked like that in months, and that I had given him the best head—"maybe ever . . . !" I blushed and said shyly, "Thanks, sweetie. I just couldn't get enough of you." We didn't leave my bedroom for an entire day.*

*Since then, even though I already knew it, I've realized that Jimmy taught me an incredibly important skill. In fact, my husband and I have been together for over ten years, and I don't think it's just because I make really good chilaquiles!*

—Theresa, thirty-seven, Hollywood

## Mutual Acquaintance Mackdowns

Most of us have friends and family members who simply *love* setting us up with those incredibly amazing, brilliant, gorgeous, rich, hilarious, sensitive, coolest-person-ever, and can't-believe-he's-single guys, right? Uh, yeah. If you don't, consider yourself lucky. Generally, it turns out that most of those adjectives don't apply, there are lots of reasons why he's single, and he should probably either stay that way or find a nice homely girl to fill the role of his new mother, er, wife.

On the other hand, there are also guys that your friends or family members know, but they would never think to set you up with *those* men. The secret? Generally, those are the guys you definitely want to score. They're totally hot but certainly not relationship material (unlike the guys they set you up with, who are probably relationship material but definitely not going to be worthwhile in the sack). Our advice: Avoid the dudes your acquaintances try to set you up with (like Helen's moister-than-a-Betty-Crocker-man, on the next page), and start looking at those guys your pals and relations never considered offering up to you instead. Hit on the latter if you find yourself in their company—and get your-

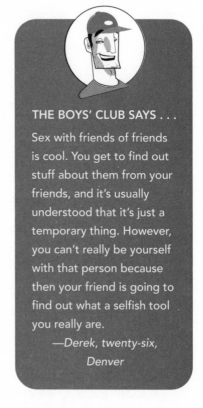

**THE BOYS' CLUB SAYS . . .**

Sex with friends of friends is cool. You get to find out stuff about them from your friends, and it's usually understood that it's just a temporary thing. However, you can't really be yourself with that person because then your friend is going to find out what a selfish tool you really are.

—*Derek, twenty-six,*
*Denver*

self the mutual acquaintance action of your dreams (we hope). See "Wedding Balls," later in the chapter, for more on the upside of this particular category.

| Ups | Downs |
| --- | --- |
| You can easily get the dirt on him from the people you trust most. | You can't trust that he won't spill the dirt on you to those people. |
| Easy to access. | Not so easy to avoid after the fact, if he's a dud. |
| Your friends or family might be psyched you got together. | Your friends or family might wonder why your standards are so low. |

## SEXCAPADE: Sweatin' to the Oldies

*I met Paul at a family barbecue a few years back. He was smart, charming, funny, and really sexy in an earthy sort of way. We spent the afternoon flirting, and we really connected. He was a doctor and worked in my dad's practice. I didn't realize it was a setup until I went to get a drink, and my dad gave me the thumbs-up. It was such a mixed moment, so sweet yet very awkward, but at least I knew Paul had my father's approval. When he walked me to my car I felt the anticipation mounting. Was he going to kiss me good night? I was so happy when he did and then asked for my number.*

*Paul called the next day, and we made a plan for that evening. I could hardly contain my excitement. Dinner was amazing. The conversation flowed, and I seriously thought that we had potential to go further, maybe even a full-on relationship. When we got back to my place, we started fooling around, and it was getting pretty hot and heavy. I asked him if he wanted to move it into my bedroom, and he agreed.*

*Once we hit the sheets, disaster ensued. He was on top of me, and when I wrapped my arms around his back, they slid off. He wasn't just perspiring a little; it was full-on flop sweat. I figured I could roll with it, maybe it would stop, or I would find it would turn me on. No go.*

*He put on the condom, and we were in missionary position. I remember looking up at him, and that's when the real waterworks began. It started dripping on me. In two minutes, I was soaking wet and so grossed out. There was no way I was going to climax, so I just prayed he would get off quickly and get out. Somehow, I made it through without drowning.*

*As I was loading my sweat-soaked sheets into the washing machine that night, I couldn't help wondering if there wasn't some prescription he could get to cure his sex sweats. Even if he could (and being a doctor, he'd probably already searched for a* 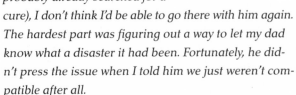 *cure), I don't think I'd be able to go there with him again. The hardest part was figuring out a way to let my dad know what a disaster it had been. Fortunately, he didn't press the issue when I told him we just weren't compatible after all.*

—Helen, twenty-seven, Destin, Florida

## Bonking Friends' Ex-Boyfriends

Okay, seriously, this is a bad idea. There's a reason your friend and this guy broke up: either because he was a dick or, well, probably because he was a dick. *Maybe* he's a great guy and things just didn't work out; perhaps he was even good in bed or had other redeeming qualities. Unfortunately, that's for your friend to know and for you to only find out from her.

This is one step away from sleeping with a guy while your friend is still with him. It's simply riddled with problems. Sure, there are always those people who will put casual sex in that "it was just sex—it didn't mean anything to me" box. But guess what? Just because casual sex doesn't mean anything other than pure, hedonistic pleasure to the parties involved doesn't mean it means nothing to the people who are on the outside looking in (like your friend whose ex you just did). The other person will infuse these things with a lot more meaning than you ever will.

On the flip side, there are a few exceptions to this rule, so if you are really (and we mean *really*) hot for the ex-lover of another, it could happen in just three easy steps (but make sure to follow them in order):

1. Figure out if doing him is even a remote possibility.

2. If it is, make sure it's been at least a year since your friend and the guy broke up.

3. Have a long chat with your friend about how she would feel if you and her ex hooked up (and make sure she's straight with you about it).

If you don't do these things, and you don't get the go-ahead, you'll potentially be down a friend—and perhaps a lot of other good friends who will stand by her—if you still opt to go for it. You dig?

| Ups | Downs |
|---|---|
| You get laid. | You lose a friend. |
| Um, you get laid? | It's so not worth it. |
| Yeah . . . that's pretty much it: You get laid. | Bad karma, dear. |

### SEXCAPADE: Good Times Gone Bad

*I had a wonderful friendship with my last roommate, Terri—in the beginning, anyway. As great as she seemed at first, the longer we lived together, the more I began to lose respect for the way she treated men. She wasn't the most honest person when it came to what she wanted. She would make a guy think she was really interested in him, and as soon as he fell for her, she would do the big blow off. Instead of calling it what it was from the beginning, or filling them in on the fact that she didn't want a relationship, she would just leave them hanging, never returning their calls. She was so cheesy, she actually started referring to herself as "Good Times Terri"—even though most guys were learning she was anything but.*

*Well, one evening I brought Terri to my ex-boyfriend Gary's party. Gary and I had remained friends, but as soon as I introduced him to Terri, it was obvious they couldn't have hated each other more. They were verbally sparring the entire evening. On the drive home, Terri asked me how I could have stayed close to an ex who was such an ass. I said I didn't think he was an ass, but "to each her own." Time passed and I found* myself having to work to keep Terri and Gary from being at the same functions or in any room together.

One night, Terri and I went to a karaoke bar for a night of drinks and bad singing. When we walked in, I knew I was in trouble: sitting at the bar was Gary. We walked over and I reintroduced them and prayed there was a table on the other side of the room from him. I went to get drinks, and when I returned, I was shocked to see that Gary and Terri were both laughing and seemed to be getting along great. I was relieved.

The night ended up being really fun for everyone. Terri and Gary actually ended up enjoying each other's company and even sang a few duets together. I was so happy that I didn't have to deal with the keep-away game anymore that I didn't see the next curveball coming: When we got home, Terri got into the house, she turned to me and asked if I would mind if she and Gary hooked up. Knowing Terri's history and Gary's pattern of wearing his heart on his sleeve, I said I didn't think it was a good idea and it would just be awkward for everyone involved if it went sour. I also pointed out that if it was something she thought was going to have a future, I couldn't really say anything, but if it was just a hook-up, I would rather she didn't. She nodded, said she understood my point, and wouldn't go there.

The next day Gary called me, and while we were chatting, he mentioned that he and Terri had made plans to watch a movie at his place that evening. He just wanted to make sure I was cool with it. I was in an awkward position—I didn't want to seem like a jealous ex, so I said it was fine and prayed that they didn't do anything beyond watching a movie.

The thing is, Terri had told me she had a pottery class that night. When she was leaving, I told her to have fun at her "class," and she replied, "I'm sure I will." I was so pissed and disappointed with her. I kept thinking, "Why ask if you're going to go behind my back and do it (and him) anyway?"

When she didn't come home that night or the next day, I drove over to Gary's to confront her. As I was driving up his street, they passed me in Gary's car. He cluelessly waved, and I was just able to make out the guiltiest look of shock on Terri's face. She was busted. Women are supposed to have each other's backs when it comes to men. I clearly would never be able to trust her again.

When Terri finally arrived home that evening, I said, "I hope it was a good time Terri—but to be honest, I think you should move out." I know it was melodramatic of me, but I was really hurt. The interesting thing is, Gary called me the next day and said that as much as he had had a good time with Terri, he really thought she was a bit psycho and he didn't want it to go any further. Terri moved out the next month, and I haven't seen her since.

—Sonja, thirty-nine, Tucson

## Revenge Is Sweet

While you should rarely, if ever, do your friend's ex, there's certainly nothing wrong with doing your ex's friend! Sure, your ex may call you a slut for sleeping with his friends, but we all know what he really means, right? (If you need an ex-boyfriend translator, here you go: "Why, oh why, did I give up that fine piece of ass?!")

## Doing Your Own Ex

Oh, this is a fun one. If you've never gone back to your ex for at least one final, genital-pounding night of hard-core action, raise your hand. We actually find it hard to believe that 31 percent of our Happy Hook-Up survey respondents say they never have. C'mon! Sex with the ex . . . ?!

We thought everyone had done it—and much as it may seem like a sign of weakness on the part of ex-girlfriends everywhere, it's not really. The truth is that women *and* men are guilty (and we use the term lightly) of going back for a little post-farewell fornication after breaking up—particularly when the sex was incredible and neither is having any success at finding anyone quite as good in bed (or is having any

sex, period). Plus, the banging is the easiest thing to reinstate—it's all the other stuff in the relationship that probably wasn't working. "The best casual sex I've ever had was mad, passionate sex with my ex-boyfriend," says Adelle, thirty-five, of Los Angeles. "Doing it as if it would be the last time to explore this wonder of attraction (which it was), ripping the clothes off and getting out all this pent-up anger, desire, and every possible feeling, just makes for the very best sex."

The interesting part of all of this is that there are a whole lot of potential pros and cons. If you're genuinely over him, but the sex was amazing, then there's a good chance you can handle it, enjoy it, and even come away from it with a certain level of empowerment (it's happened to the best of us). On the other hand, if you have any illusions (actually *delusions*) that jumping back into bed together will undo all the hurt and rebuild the shattered remnants of your long-gone, never-coming-back-again relationship—dig a little deeper, sweetheart. "My biggest shouldn't is ex-boyfriends," says Emily, twenty-three, of Chapel Hill, North Carolina. "You broke up for a reason, but sex really makes that reason less clear. Next thing you know, you think you want him back but you really don't—it's only the sex. Then you get into the really bad part of wanting him back when he doesn't want you, or vice versa. That is always ugly. Somebody comes out a loser and the other on top."

So if you think you're going to wind up wanting him back after enjoying one more serving at the ex-boyfriend buffet, turn back to chapter 1 and start learning your casual sex lessons all over. Remember: when it comes to happy hook-ups, no emotions or expectations allowed!

| Ups | Downs |
| --- | --- |
| So you lost the love—but the sex is still great. | Great sex can make you wish you were still in love. |
| Ain't nothing wrong with a farewell fuck. | Sometimes you wind up getting farewell fucked. |
| You can prove to yourself that you can use him for sex. | You wind up feeling like you've been used for sex. |

## SEXCAPADE: Don't Mess with Exes

*Kevin and I had an amazing on-again, off-again relationship for three years. We loved and respected each other's space, hardly ever fought, and to be perfectly honest, the sex was the best I've ever had. We had this unexplainable connection in the bedroom, or wherever we landed, that defied any sort of logic. We always said, "We just fit."*

*The main reason it was as much off as on, from what I could figure, was that he had a lot of personal demons and battled with a bit of depression. The first time we split up was for six weeks; then we got together for a drink, to talk, and ended up back in his bed. The bad pattern was set. I should have been stronger and insisted he deal with his shit. But I didn't say anything. My bad.*

*A year passed, and all was good with us—or so I thought. As time went on, I noticed he was becoming distant and moody. He'd go to work, get home, call me to chat for a while, then hang up and sit on the couch all night, watching TV. He was unmotivated. If I hadn't made plans for us on the weekends or various nights during the week, he probably would have never left the couch except for work. When we did go out, we always had fun and laughed our asses off. Everything was good, especially the sex, but left alone he would spiral.*

*He kept saying he wasn't sure where he was going or what he wanted in the future. I tried to help him by encouraging him to talk with his friends and family, if he wasn't comfortable talking to me. I even suggested he go talk it through with his therapist, but he rarely did.*

*True to form, another year in, he broke up with me again. I was kicking myself, I was so distraught, and I really tried my best to stay away. But three months later, we slept together, and I was once again hooked. The thing that really sucked was that he was able to separate his emotions from the act, and I wasn't. It was all casual good times for him, and I was the one who ended up heartbroken and disappointed.*

*Fortunately, I finally realized he wasn't the right guy for me to be in a relationship with—let alone near a bed with—and I've successfully kept my distance for over a year. I'm even seeing new people. Wish me luck.*

—Corrina, thirty-nine, Falmouth, Massachusetts

## Neighborly Nookie

So maybe exes aren't the best-case scenario—certainly not after repeated attempts and the whole "are we or aren't we?" confusion. Hey, that's reason enough to start checking out the gorgeous dude next door (if such a guy exists). We heard Ruth's rant on this subject, and it sure wasn't Mr. Rogers–rated, but here's the thing: it's incredibly tough to resist going at it with a big, hot stud who has just moved in—or perhaps you're the one who has crash-landed in lovin' land. Hell, maybe you've lived in close proximity to each other for ages and only recently noticed how much the cutie round the corner has going on, or vice versa.

Regardless, what they say about property can also be true for casual sex. Uh huh, that's right: it's all about location, location, location. And as with exes, doing the hottie in the 'hood is loaded with pros and cons. Oh, stop your whining. We're just saying it's worth wondering how hard it might be to stay away from each other (as

many women will tell you, the more times you sleep with someone, the less likely it's going to remain casual). Then, you've got to figure out how you're going to feel if you see him with another woman; after all, you've got the vantage point, and there's a fine line between being a sweet neighbor next door and being a scary stalker slapped with a restraining order (that goes for you . . . him . . . maybe both). So weigh it carefully.

| Ups | Downs |
| --- | --- |
| He's next door when you need him. | He's next door when you *don't*. |
| You can keep tabs on his every move. | Some moves shouldn't be observed so closely. |
| You can certainly borrow his sugar. | Too much sugar, and you're left with a bunch of rotten teeth. |

## SEXCAPADE: A Moving Experience

*I was walking my dog home from the park one day, and around the corner from my house, I saw a moving truck. I slowed down to see who was moving into or out of the neighborhood and was happy to see two really hot guys coming down the stairs. I let my dog nose around on their lawn, hoping they would come over and introduce themselves. It didn't take long for both of them to notice me and come over to meet me and, of course, my dog.*

*They told me they had just moved to the big city from a very small farming community in Iowa. They were both really cute and sweet, but I couldn't help feeling that there was some amazing attraction between myself and one of the guys. His name was Risk, kind of a weird name for a Midwestern farm boy, but I was ready to take one with him (ba-dum-bum). He had a really sweet smile, huge dimples, and the darkest brown bedroom eyes I'd ever seen. We stood in his yard for a while, flirting and getting to know each other, and I finally asked if he'd like a tour of the city the next day. I swear, he said, "That would be just swell." In most situations, I would've turned and run for the hills if a guy used the word "swell," but he was so genuine and sincere, and frankly, his Podunk drawl was actually turning me on.*

*The next day, Risk walked around the corner to pick me up. We drove around all the funky neighborhoods, and I pointed out the hot spots. I kept looking over at him, and his jaw was dropped and his eyes were popping wide open. "I've never seen anything like this in my whole darn life" was all he kept saying. He was so green, like a kid at Disneyland for the first time.*

*I ended the tour with sunset down at the beach. He went to give me an innocent thank you hug and kiss while the sun went down, and we ended up lip-locked and wildly making out. I'm not sure who taught him his technique, but I must thank the gals in Iowa for their training. He was an amazing kisser. Soft and gentle at first, then he totally took control and got me so hot, I was willing to drop down and do him right there. He was such a gentleman. He said, "Maybe we should go someplace more private. I don't want you like this, I want to be able to spend quality time on you." I'd hit gold! Take time on me . . . yes, please!*

*I drove us back to my place, at top speed, and when we got into the entrance hall of my apartment, he was going down on me before I knew what hit me. The shy guy was gone, and he was a master at the craft of cunnilingus. I climaxed so hard, I was sure all my neighbors heard. I didn't care, though; all I wanted was more of him.*

*We only made it halfway up the stairs before I went down on him. He tasted so sweet, and I loved his reaction to what I was doing. It just turned me on even more. I didn't want him to climax before I was able to get him in me, so I suggested we stop for a moment and move to my bed.*

*Once there, he went for another trip down south. By the time we had the condom on him and he was in me, I had come again. He gave me the ride of a lifetime, and when he and I had climaxed for the last time, he gently kissed me on the cheek, thanked me for the tour of the city and of my body, put on his Wranglers, and left. I was lying there in that great post-sex haze, wondering when I'd next see Risk—if it would be awkward or not.*

*Cut to two days later. I'm getting in my car, and I see a note on my windshield: "I can't thank you enough for your intro to the city. If you ever want to discover new neighborhoods with me in the future, I am available. If not, no worries. I'm sure I'll find another tour guide someday; she just won't taste as good as you. I am around the corner, literally. Signed, Risk"*

*God, he was good. I was at his place in record time. We kept getting together randomly for a few months, each time was hot sex and a very standard "Thanks, see ya." Then, one Sunday morning, I saw him in the neighborhood café, gazing intensely into another girl's eyes as he held her hand. I was a little disappointed, but realized it was what it was. We'd both gotten what we needed. Plus, if things didn't work out with his latest girl, he knew where to find me.*

—Bonnie, thirty-nine, San Diego

## Workplace Whoopie

Talk about the ultimate sticky situation. We all have to work, and we all want to play, but playing around with a coworker can be dangerous. Of course, there are those rare occasions where romance blooms in the workplace—after all, you spend a huge chunk of your life there, so it can be a decent place to meet a mate. But, developing a long-term relationship with a man from the office is very different from shtooping the cutie in the next cubicle, with no plans to make it permanent.

Sure, the naughty factor can be a huge turn-on, but the day-to-day relationship—not to mention the job itself—can suffer if the cards aren't laid down on the proverbial table (or in this case, desk). We're not saying you absolutely shouldn't go there, because let's face it, you probably will anyway, but don't forget that this is one case where there's no escaping the inevitable. You will see him the next day at the watercooler . . . and in the elevator . . . and in the hallway . . . and so on. "If you have casual sex with a friend, neighbor, or coworker, even if it doesn't change your relationship much, it will make you overanalyze everything you say and everything he says, forever after," points out Marsha, thirty-five, of Saratoga, New York. "And it stings a little when he's ogling other girls."

Beyond that, people always find out. Word spreads, and particularly if your coworkers don't have lives of their own, they'll use you to keep the tedium of their miserable existences interesting. Suddenly, you're the hot gossip topic of the week, if not the month or year. If you don't mind being known as the girl who blew the intern in the supply closet, after-hours, then more power to you. If you're willing to lose your job over it (many employers actually have policies against this sort of thing), keep on going, honey. On the other hand, if you're not interested in facing the possible consequences, it would be worth your while to steer clear of casual sex with your colleagues, or, at the very least, be discreet about it. After all, if you don't keep it classified, you may find yourself perusing the classifieds.

| Ups | Downs |
| --- | --- |
| You can make him your sexual apprentice. | Do the words "you're fired!" mean anything to you? |
| It breaks up the office tedium. | It breaks up the office tedium for everyone else, too. |
| Doing it on the reception desk or in the elevator can be hot, hot, hot. | The screening session of the secret camera footage with HR—not so hot. |

## SEXCAPADE: Occupational Hazard

*I started a new job about a month or two before the holidays. There was this incredibly cute guy working upstairs. I always clammed up whenever I saw him and wondered if I'd ever get the opportunity to talk to him.*

*Then, as luck would have it, he was invited to our office Christmas party. After several celebratory cocktails, I wound up in the same general vicinity as him, and soon we were in one big group of people talking about something or other. I kept giving him these longing looks. Finally, we were introduced by some of the other coworkers, and we wound up off in a corner, talking with each other. I couldn't tell if he was into me or not. Then, we wound up in the same car, getting a ride home. He and I were sitting next to each other. When we got to his place, some of the girls from the office told him to give me a peck good night, so he did (albeit awkwardly).*

*Somehow, I got it into my head that we'd had some magic moment. The next day at work, in my hungover stupor, I decided to leave him a little note before heading out for vacation. It said something like, "Give me a call over the holidays if you like—I'm always up for a good time." Pathetic. Every time the phone rang for the next few days, I jumped, wondering if it was him. I was so nervous! What would I say if he actually called? Finally, he did call, but I wasn't home. He left a somewhat awkward message. I called him back and left an equally awkward message. We never wound up speaking.*

*Back at the office a couple of weeks later, we wound up in the elevator together, and he literally would not even acknowledge me or look in my direction. After that, any time we wound*

*up passing each other in the halls or anything, he wouldn't speak to me and I wouldn't speak to him. He would just look really uncomfortable. I would get nervous and awkward and run away. To this day, I'm certain it's because I spooked him so badly! The saddest part is nothing even happened. What a joke.*
—Louisa, twenty-six, Springfield, Virginia

## Getting Serviced

Now we're talking. Think about how many male service providers are working right around the corner, down the street, around town—bartenders (we've certainly heard plenty of stories about these beverage-pouring boys), gardeners, grocery store checkers, cable guys, pizza deliverymen, your mechanic—they're everywhere! Plus, they're essentially at your mercy because it's your patronage that pays their bills. In a way, you're practically their sugar mama. Sure, there are downsides to doing, say, the delivery boy . . . particularly if things go wrong. (Is that extra cream in the linguini with clam sauce, or . . . ?) But in most cases, the good news is that there's more than one business in town, so you can simply change your service. Isn't capitalism great?

| Ups | Downs |
| --- | --- |
| They're used to being given orders by you. | You have to give them too many orders. |
| You're sure to get service that makes you smile. | If the service is bad, you've got to change your provider. |
| Perhaps a discount in the future? | Perhaps you'll end up discontinued in the future. |

## Celebrity Screws

We admit it may be a long shot that the person you see on the
big or small screen (or, more than likely, rocking out at your local club
or scoring a touchdown at the sports arena) will be a sure thing for
shagging—but you never know. In fact, whether you live in Manhattan
or Middle America, there are always stars—A-list or otherwise—that

venture into cities big and small. Brace yourself if they do because, yes, they really are easy. At least, that's been our experience. Even the ones whom you believe to be tied down are not necessarily faithful; because they can pretty much sleep with anyone they want, they often do. It may not be true of all of them, but trust us—it's true of a lot of them. We certainly can't name any names, as they have lawyers that are just as powerful as their libidos. But suffice to say, celebrities, particularly because many high-profile males are of the alpha male variety, are the sluttiest of them all.

| Ups | Downs |
| --- | --- |
| Lots of experience = potential for skillful sex. | Lots of experience = potential for scary STDs. |
| Recognizable, so probably safe to screw. | Recognizable, so you'll see them everywhere after the fact (just not with you). |
| You hear they're great in bed and ready for action. | You can't believe everything you hear. |

## SEXCAPADE: See You Around

*I once got together with this guy who used to be on a soap opera. The sex was really good, and we wound up having a few booty calls for about a month or so. Then we just lost touch. I wasn't really familiar with his work (if you can call it that), but one night, I turned on the TV, and there he was on some new sitcom. I couldn't believe it! Then, about a month later, I was flipping through the cable channels, and there he was again, in some movie I'd never heard of. I swear, for the next year at least, it seemed like every few weeks, I would turn on the TV and see this guy somewhere else. It was kind of cool to realize I'd slept with someone who was sort of a celebrity. At the same time, it was kind of a pain, because every time I saw him on TV, I realized that was going to be my only real opportunity to see him, since the sex was no more. Bummer.*

—Tanita, thirty-six, Nashville

## Ho'ing with a Husband

If you're seriously thinking that the guy dragging around the ball and chain is going to be a prime candidate for getting you off—well, yes and no. We do appreciate the fact that you're willing to go for someone who's so completely unavailable, there's no way in hell you'd become emotionally attached (right?). Then again, as with the ex-boyfriend-of-a-friend situation, you're sowing some seriously bad karma for yourself here. As we said, even though in your mind—and his—you're just scratching an itch, and you're not in love, any sex you have with someone else's man is going to be perceived as meaning a lot more to the two of you than it actually does, whether they're a happy couple or not.

Who cares if you don't know his wife? Who cares if he's the one to blame for cheating on her? Are you really going to try to use that old "he's coming to me because he's not getting what he needs at home" line on us? Please. Get over yourself, honey, and don't go there. Maybe you're not technically a home wrecker, but you certainly operated the equipment that brought the house down on some level. Above all, don't do him in his own damn bed. "Never sleep in the bed of a married man. (You never know when his wife might walk in!)," agrees sex columnist and author Anka Radakovich. We'll take that one step further and say, just don't sleep with him in any bed, period. Honestly.

| Ups | Downs |
|---|---|
| It's so damn forbidden, it really turns you on. | It's so damn forbidden, it's actually against the law. |
| You know he's not going to keep calling you. | His wife might be the one calling—or even kicking your ass. |
| You get to feel like the other woman, the one who really knows how to screw him. | You get to feel like the other woman, the one who screws over other women. |

### SEXCAPADE: Fatal Attraction

*I was working on this really low budget movie as a production assistant, and the first day of the shoot I saw him: Brad, the second assistant director. He was killer hot. Not a model type, much earthier and scruffier, in an unshaved geeky kind of way. Normally, I'm the laziest worker ever, but when I woke up the second day of the shoot, all I could think was, "I get to see Brad today!" I was actually ten minutes early for call time.*

*We spent the first few hours checking each other out, and by the time we broke for lunch, I knew he was into me. That afternoon, we caught each other's eye whenever possible, and every time, I would slyly smile and hope he was getting my message. We kept this up for the next few days, not really talking, but oh was there some crazy chemistry. I wanted him in a bad, bad way. At one point, he asked me if he could borrow a pen, and when I handed it to him, he took the time to touch my hand in that "I wanted to touch you" way. Serious waves of wanting washed over me. I was fantasizing about being with him, not in a boyfriend/girlfriend way, but in a "do me, right here, today" way.*

*Later that day, I was talking with the props girl and gossiping about the people on our crew, and she said she had worked with Brad on another film. I didn't want to tip her off too much, so I nonchalantly asked what his deal was. "Oh, he's married and has two kids. I think his daughter is turning two this week," she said. I was stunned silent. What was he doing? What was he thinking? I am not that kind of girl. I was sick to my stomach. All I kept thinking was, "Did he think I was going to be another notch on his set tools belt?"*

*I instantly lost my attraction for Brad, but I was in this terribly awkward position. How the hell was I going to get through eight more weeks with him? When he approached me the next day and tried to be all flirty, I looked directly into his eyes and said, "I hear you've got a little girl who's turning two soon— that's so great." He immediately knew the gig was up. He stammered a little and admitted that he and his wife were still working on finding a clown for the party. I said, "Not that I believe in typecasting, but maybe you should take that gig." I've got to give the man snaps for realizing he was busted and didn't have a shot in hell at cheating on his wife or family with me.*

*The pathetic thing is that I kept catching him checking me out on set, straight on through to the end of the filming. So cute, so smart—and yet so ridiculously stupid.*

—Christy, thirty-eight, Los Angeles

See? Christy's got common sense, and she handled that sticky situation with the right kind of attitude ... so her conscience is clear. Our little friend Suzie might be well served to take a page from Christy's book. Not that we're judging; we're pretty sure instant karma will take care of this home wrecker:

## SEXCAPADE: Ooh Ooh, Witchy Woman

*Married men turn out to be the most ideal candidates for casual sex. Don't get me wrong; I don't think it's a good idea to fool around with married men at all.* [Authors' Note: Uh huh.] *My luck is just that the guys who seem sexy and interesting often end up being married—and they don't always let me know that information right away.* [Authors' Note: Fascinating.] *But guys who are in town for a few weeks on business often end up being married and often end up being whom I would have casual sex with. Whether or not that's ideal, that's another story.* [Authors' Note: Do tell.] *I do think it's better than trying that with a friend or neighbor who will still be around, because chances are he'll start dating or sleeping with someone else, and I'll be hurt. Even if I didn't get emotionally attached to him, I'll wonder what was it about me that made him go on to someone else instead.* [Authors' Note: Better that someone's wife get hurt than you, right? Get back to us when you're hitched. Thanks.]

—Suzie, thirty-two, Montgomery, Alabama

## Lesbo Lust

We've already gone over the friends-who-screw scenario, and it bears repeating that if you're going to do it with one of your best buddies, the chances are good that you might just destroy that friendship—and that's whether we're talking a male or female friend. Of course, there are other ladies who fall into various categories—the ones you meet at bars, the friends of friends, maybe even the service providers, or married women. So, when you're reading up on all of these other scenarios, consider that the females will also carry most of the same pros and cons.

Outside of all that, what we'd really like to say is this: if you consider yourself to be a straight girl, but you want to see how the muff-divers live and there appear to be more pros than cons in doing so, then more power to you. There are a number of reasons why this could work and, of course, a few reasons why it may not.

On the upside: if you truly believe yourself to be hetero, chances are you're not going to become emotionally attached to a woman or want a serious relationship with her. Bonus! Plus, when it comes to girl-on-girl action, most women say that your chances of getting off are increased greatly ("We tend to know what we want and what feels good, whether we're giving or receiving," confirms Sonja, twenty-four, of Washington, D.C.). Third, no matter how many strides have been made in ridding society of homophobia, it's got to be said that there's still something slightly taboo about a same-sex encounter, and while that's unfortunate, it also makes it even hotter. In a nutshell (without the nuts): you've got a lot of good stuff here.

Of course, if you've bought into any of the social stigmas society likes to thrust on homosexuals, then you may be playing with a fire you don't know how to put out ("Oh my God! Does this mean I'm g-g-g-gay?!")—but then again, maybe the encounter will give you exactly the mind-expanding opportunity you need.

| Ups | Downs |
| --- | --- |
| Taboos can be a real turn-on. | Taboos can create a lot of confusion. |
| You don't need to instruct her. | She might have to instruct you. |
| Lesbians can be hot! | Butch dykes can be scary! |

## SEXCAPADE: Fantasy Island

*I swear this is true . . . I know it's gonna sound like a made-up Penthouse Forum tale, but it really did happen. A few years ago, some girls I was working with at Hooters (believe it or not) and I took a road trip down to Mexico for a long weekend. In the car on the way down, the subject of kissing came up, and three of the five of us admitted to kissing or making out with another girl. I figured all of us had, but two of the girls—Lori and Michelle—said they hadn't and would never want to. And while I admitted to kissing a girl, the other two—Carly and Paula—said they had gone even farther than that. Lori and Michelle were so shocked and grossed out that I started feeling a bit judged (even though I hadn't gone as far as the other two). So, I quickly changed the subject and hoped it wouldn't be brought up again.*

*When we got to the trailer we were staying in (yes, trailer), we unpacked, threw on our suits, and hit the beach. That night we went to the bars in town. We danced for hours, and after fighting off the local men, we bought a bottle of tequila and headed home to hang out and play cards. We were playing poker and drinking margaritas when the kissing subject was brought up again. When Paula dared Lori to kiss me, I figured Lori would freak out again and say no go, but she leaned in and planted one on me! I must admit I was totally turned on. The kiss and the amount of tequila in our systems broke the ice, and suddenly it was a full-on make-out session.*

*At one point, I was kissing and grinding with Paula, and out of the corner of my eye, I caught a glimpse of Lori and Michelle going at it. I was so shocked, I started giggling and pointed it out to Paula, who laughed and said, "I'm so not surprised; they just needed a little encouragement and a lot of tequila." That night I had my first girl-on-girl(s) experience! I wouldn't say I'm a lesbian, but I've always been curious, and I will say I had a really great time.*

*Of course, there was a bit of embarrassment the next morning. Lori and Michelle, in particular, could hardly look at each other, but in time, I knew they would move on and get over it. At least I hoped they would.*

—Mandi, thirty-two, Encinitas, California

## Orgy Explosions

If you're hooking up with one person who knows one or more people who might want to join the party, then that could potentially be an amazing opportunity to increase your sexual satisfaction exponentially, right? That depends. We all know the cliché about the biggest male fantasy: having two women at once. Sometimes it's a woman's biggest fantasy, too (as we witnessed in Mandi's Hooters ho-down, above).

**THE BOYS' CLUB SAYS . . .**

My most disappointing casual sex was the old trio con brio: my girlfriend at the time plus a girl I was madly in love with all through college. It wasn't sexually disappointing, just emotionally very volatile and, ultimately, sad.

—*Chris, forty-one,*
*La Jolla, California*

"My best casual sex experience was with my husband and a good friend of ours," adds Liza, twenty-eight, of Hollywood. Meegan, twenty-four, of New York City, is yet another fan of group sex: "On my friend's twenty-sixth birthday, we had a six-some orgy in my closet, to help him celebrate. It was him with five women—and my first oral sex with a woman. Very special indeed," she reveals.

Depending on how many people are involved and who they are, group sex could be your opportunity to try out a lot more than you ever imagined, same sex or otherwise. If our Happy Hook-Up survey is anything to go by, 19 percent of the women and 37 percent of the men agree (that was the percentage of respondents claiming to have had group sex at least once).

That said, this is one of those situations you want to think through even more carefully than the typical casual sex scenario. While doing multiple people at once can be interesting and exciting, it can also be followed by embarrassment and awkwardness—particularly if the odds are good that you'll be seeing any of these people again. (Again, review Mandi's story above.)

To avoid any discomfort, you should be sure to make this decision when you're in a rational head-space, and do it with people with whom you feel completely comfortable and with whom jealousy and weirdness won't be the end result. "If you're going to hook up with a lot of people at once, you've got to be doing this for sport and not just because you're high or something," says Deanna, forty, of Los Angeles. "There's no room for egos, no room for guilt, no room for anything but being certain you want to be there and you want to get off. If you have any reservations about doing this kind of thing—and I mean *any* reservations—you should probably just stick with watching it on a video. It's not for everyone."

| Ups | Downs |
| --- | --- |
| It can get pretty hot being touched and fondled by many at the same time. | Many people can equal much confusion. |
| The more the merrier. | The more people you have to face later. |
| If one person isn't getting you off, maybe someone else will. | You may be expected to get many off in the process—no rest for the weary! |

**bicurious,** *adj.* (also see "heteroflexible"), a person who may seem gay—and even indulge in a same-sex encounter once in a while—but who still considers herself to be straight

e.g., "Catherine got together with Amanda last night, but she says she's just exploring her bicurious tendencies."

**ambisextrous,** *adj.*, ability to swing both ways; bisexual

e.g., "Sam is ambisextrous; he slept with Carol last week and George last night."

**bibe,** *n.*, an aura of bisexuality, as in a bisexual vibe

e.g., "She looked straight, but when she felt her friend's ass, I got a definite bibe from her."

**trisexual,** *n.*, a person who will "tri" anything sexual at least once

e.g., "Sure, I'll do anal, lesbian, straight, threesomes—whatever. I am trisexual, after all."

**heteroflexible,** *adj.* (also see "bicurious"), predominantly heterosexual, but may sample the same-sex waters on occasion.

e.g., "Sally is generally all about the cock, but when she got trashed the other night and went down on Amanda, she discovered her heteroflexible tendencies."

**homoflexible,** *adj.*, predominantly homosexual, but may sample the opposite-sex waters on occasion.

e.g., "Joshua was in a long-term relationship with Jacob, but now he's sleeping with Jezebel. I guess he's homoflexible."

# Oh, the Places You'll Go

Now that we've run through the various people in your life, let's venture on over to the different locations where you might be able to home in on a hook-up. Sure, there's always the usual bar scene, which can be an excellent bet (with some downsides of course), as well as the supermarket, the Laundromat, and many others. Beyond your local liaisons, you've also got opportunities galore when you get away from it all. So now we'll get to most of those, and let you in on what to expect and be aware of.

## Bar Banging

Practically everyone who has casual sex meets at least one conquest at a watering hole or some sort of club where alcohol abounds. It's a bit of a no-brainer: when you drink, you feel sexy, people look sexy, and before you know it, you're all feeling sexy together and the fornication soon follows. What could possibly be wrong with that situation? Well, we already addressed it to a degree in chapter 3: When you mix alcohol with action, the extreme inebriation that can and does happen can seriously cloud your judgment. Suddenly, a grotesquely unattractive guy morphs into a demigod before your very eyes, or you simply wind up making really bad decisions. For instance, "Sure, I'd love to come back to your frat house!" "Okay, I'll have anal sex with you!" "No, don't worry about the condoms—I'm on the pill." You get the picture.

On the other hand, if you follow the stay-relatively-sober rule, you might just wind up meeting the one-night man of your dreams— and any bar will do. If you like pilots, head out to one near the airport; if you want to do a suit, head downtown or wherever the businessmen hang out; if you like them a little scruffy, a dive with a pool table is your best bet. Find the ones where the competition won't be as stiff (so to speak)—for instance, happy hour in the financial district.

The great thing is that when you take a guy home with you from a bar (generally the best way to go; you don't want to get stranded at this random guy's place, but see chapter 7 for more on this subject), it's a given that you are simply getting together for a casual screw. Your expectations and his should remain relatively low simply because of the scenario in which you meet. Plus, if you start feeling a little weird about it the next day, just pretend you were way more trashed than you already were. Everyone loves (and forgives) a lush— even the Lord. As long as you're sober, it's all good: no expectations, no explanations necessary. Go out, have fun, get rid of him, and boom—you're done.

| Ups | Downs |
| --- | --- |
| Alcohol is readily available and lowers your inhibitions. | Too much alcohol and you lose all inhibitions. |
| Lots of drinks followed by fornication! | Fornication followed by hangover! |
| Bars can be dark, mysterious, and inviting environments. | Then there's seeing him in the harsh light of day. |

## SEXCAPADE: A Toast to My Future

*On my twenty-third birthday, I had recently broken up with my boyfriend, and I was feeling happy to be rid of him and quite full of myself. I went out in a fabulous outfit with my friends to celebrate. We were all dressed to kill, and I had little bottles of alcohol in my purse that I handed out at the bar we went to.*

*While my friends were dancing and making spectacles of themselves, a very handsome boy asked me to dance. That never happens. Usually it's the guy you don't want to dance with that asks you. So, yes, we danced and danced, and as the night wore on and the bar was closing, I asked him to go with my friends and me to another bar I knew of that stayed open after-hours. He agreed.*

*At the next bar, this scary guy tried to flirt with me—at which point I asked my cute new friend to kiss me, so the other guy would leave. He did, and it was amazing. Finally, we decided we should probably move our make-out session to a more private location. We went back to my apartment and had a great night of sex. I even made him go to a local liquor store at 3 A.M. to get more condoms, which he gladly did. Anyway, this night turned out to be one to remember . . . as I ended up marrying him!*

—Marjorie, forty-four, Indianapolis

## Fluff and Fold Fun

Ahhh, the Laundromat—what better place for some good, clean fun? Nothing says casual sex like dryer sheets, detergent, and dudes darning their socks, right? Since single people often live in apartments, and since apartments often don't have washing machines and dryers, you're bound to find lots of eligible bachelors at your local coin-op. Not only are they single, but these guys actually wash their clothes, so they've already scored two points on the do-him-now dance card.

The way we see it, there are very few minuses to a little over-the-hamper hook-up. Things to consider, though: the bright neon Laundromat lights aren't always flattering, nor do they set the perfect mood. Plus, if you do find yourself in the mood, you're going to have to leave your stuff there to potentially get stolen or haul it away with you. And by the time you make it back to the place and get your clean sheets on the bed, the desire to do each other may have subsided. Of course, there's also the possibility this guy will be a clean freak (see the "Mr. Clean" Sexcapade that follows). And finally, as with the neighborly nookie, there's always that chance that you're going to run into your local laundry-doing dude every time you run out of clean jeans.

| Ups | Downs |
| --- | --- |
| You can woo him when you pull your black thong from the dryer. | You want to run for the hills when he pulls *his* black thong from the dryer. |
| At least you know his laundry's not dirty. | Just hope he doesn't air your dirty laundry after the deed's done. |
| There's nothing like doing it on fresh, clean sheets . . . | . . . except now you have to wash them again. |

### SEXCAPADE: **Mr. Clean**

*One time I was at the Laundromat, doing my weekly wash, when I spotted this really hot guy folding his clothes. We kept eyeing each other until finally he came over and introduced himself. His name was Mark. He was tall, dark, and had these insane lips. We both knew what we wanted, and so after chatting over our hampers while our stuff dried, we headed back to my place.*

*We had amazing sex, but then things took a weird turn. After we both climaxed, he asked if he could take a shower. I said of course and gave him a freshly laundered towel. He went in, and I got into bed. I figured maybe after the shower we'd head into round two. I fell into a light sleep, and then I heard a knock on my door. It was my roommate; she just got home and had to pee. I looked at my clock and realized that Mark had been in the shower for over twenty minutes. I started to get concerned and knocked on the bathroom door. I got no response.*

*I started getting a bit freaked out, as did Connie. Did he fall and hurt himself? I didn't want to be rude, but I was really concerned. I opened the door a crack and peeked in. There he was, sitting on the floor of the shower stall, letting the water run over himself. "I'm fine," he said. "Okay," I awkwardly responded. I closed the door and told Connie he would be right out.*

*I swear another ten minutes went by, and he was still in there with the water running. Connie and I both agreed that it was not only rude but also a bit creepy. I couldn't help wondering if it was because he thought sex was dirty or, worse, that I was dirty. I was sort of amused that this all happened immediately after meeting at a Laundromat, of all places! When he finally emerged from the bathroom, I knew that I just wanted him to leave. So, I handed him his clothes and sent him on his way.*

*Cut to about a year later: I'm out with the gals from the office, and we're swapping sex stories. My coworker Linda starts telling her tale of a guy taking an extremely long shower after they'd had sex. She had the same reaction I did. "Was it me? Does he think I'm dirty?" I asked Linda his name, and*

*when she said Mark, I burst out laughing. It was the same guy.*
*At least we could be assured we weren't the dirty ones. He had*
*some serious issues with sex—not to mention sanitation.*

—Gabby, forty-one, Boise, Idaho

## Café Coitus

Wherever there's a cup of jo brewing, chances are there are some smokin' hot Joes or Johns or Bills or Brads or Toms, too. While there's less of a guarantee that all the available men will be flocking to the nearest coffeehouse, there's a good chance you'll be able to spot the ones who aren't taken. How? Boyfriends and girlfriends, married couples, and people who are dating just love to get together to feed their java fix. So, basically, all you need to do is scope the place out for the boys without a partner, and the party might just start percolating. Basically, it's a whole lot of bonuses and not much in the way of bad stuff.

| Ups | Downs |
|---|---|
| Cool people hang out at cafés. | Recovering addicts also hang out at cafés. |
| Caffeine gives you energy for action. | Too much caffeine and you'll be bouncing off the walls. |
| You can spend a long time relaxing and checking out the scene. | You can spend a long time waiting for a scene to arrive. |

## Party Penetration

Meeting a man at a swinging soirée is just about the best possible way to find a transient tryst. This situation generally comes with all the benefits of the friend-of-a-friend or family friend scenario described earlier in the chapter because, chances are, you and the guy with whom you'll go for it both know someone at the shindig. Meanwhile, everyone's in a festive mood, the libations are flowing, and so long as you heed our don't-go-beyond-a-pleasant-buzz alcohol advice, you're pretty much golden.

| Ups | Downs |
| --- | --- |
| Everyone's in the mood to raise a glass. | Too much toasting can get you toasted. |
| Easy environment for relaxed pre-sex chat. | Hard environment to lose a loser. |
| Life is a party—at least for the evening. | Some parties end sooner than we'd like them to. |

## SEXCAPADE: All Aboard

*I became friends with this hot pro skateboarder through mutual pals. The first time we met was at a barbecue. We talked a lot, and there was so much sexual tension between us, it was unbearable! I saw him again a few months later at a skateboarding contest (I worked in the industry), and afterwards, we went to a party where we drank whiskey and talked about everything in the world. It was a big party and we were holding hands and being made fun of by all our "coworkers." We didn't care.*

*We left the party and had the hottest make-out ever—on the Pacific Coast Highway, on the sidewalk. Eventually, we made it back to the hotel (lips locked the whole way) and continued to fool around. We had amazing sex while being surrounded by about five drunk and sleeping boys—a little bit dangerous. We ended up in the shower. The next day, we just lay around. He gave me his number, and we drunk dialed each other a few times, but we never wound up hooking up again. Probably for the best, but I'd still be up for it if we ever crossed paths again.*

—Darla, twenty-four, Redondo Beach, California

## Pumping and Grinding

Back in the eighties, the gym was considered the ultimate meet market—remember that cheesy John Travolta and Jamie Lee Curtis movie, *Perfect*? These days, it's eerily similar. Yes, people are still wearing spandex, dancing to bad music in the aerobics room, the guys lifting weights can be as dumb as clubs, and so on and so on. Basically, it's a great opportunity for casual sex! After all, who wouldn't want to hook up with a guy with maximum muscle mass? He's hot. Of course, he knows that—which can often be a pain. But, if it's just for a fleeting fuck, it's pretty easy to ignore the fact that he's a moronic, narcissistic Neanderthal man, and just use him like the tool that he is. Just remember that if your options for places to exercise are limited, you're going to have to deal with running into this guy as often as your workout program dictates. On the upside, since he's so into himself, chances are he won't even notice you after the deed's been done.

| Ups | Downs |
| --- | --- |
| A big, buff body | Doesn't always mean a big, buff boner (steroids, anyone?) |
| Doing a dumb guy keeps your expectations in check. | Doing a dumb guy may also keep your orgasms in check. |
| He really knows how to take care of himself. | There's a good chance that that's about all he'll take care of. |

## Shopping and Shagging

Everybody's got to eat and a lot of single guys hit the grocery store solo. It's really as simple as bumping your shopping cart into his or fondling a piece of produce as you look longingly in his direction.

Another great thing about the grocery store is that there are a million opportunities for you to start up a conversation with the guy. More and more men are taking an interest in cooking these days, so it's perfectly natural for you to approach the object of your desire and ask something along the lines of, "Do you know how to tell when bananas are ripe?" or "Any idea where the sausage is in this place?"

| Ups | Downs |
| --- | --- |
| You can wander the aisles looking for a catch of the day. | You may need to shop around for a new grocery store if his performance in the sack is fishy. |
| You get to learn a bit about him by looking in his basket. | He gets to see the Midol, Pepto, or tampons in your basket. |
| The produce and pet food aisles are great places to start up a conversation . . . | . . . Until he tells you that squash gives him the runs, or mentions he's got seventeen cats and offers to name one after you. |

## Foreign Affairs

¡Hola! Let us count the many reasons why sleeping with a guy on nondomestic soil is quite possibly the best way to go when it comes to casual sex. First of all, unless you plan on moving to this particular location, you *never* have to see him again. Furthermore, there's little need for dealing with pleasantries, particularly if you don't speak each other's language—we all know the only real language that matters, right? You can simply go for what you want and be as adventurous as you damn well please. The mere fact that you're far from home may just help you to unleash that carnal-crazy girl within that you've always wanted to come out and play. After you've had your way with him, you can get up and go and never look back—no need to exchange numbers or worry about further contact.

| Ups | Downs |
| --- | --- |
| The sex can be great when there's a language barrier and you must rely on body language. | The sex can suck when there's a language barrier and he can't read your body language. |
| Excitement of exotic locations. | Excitement of exotic STDs. |
| Fucking a foreigner is fucking amazing. | The locals just don't do it for you anymore—and now you really know what you've been missing. |

## SEXCAPADE: Italian Spice

*Ten years ago, for my college graduation, my parents announced they were taking me to Europe as my graduation gift. "Great," I thought. "Just what I need: a trip to some of the most romantic cities in the world with my folks."*

*After a week of castle tours through England, Spain, and France with a group of retired oldies from the Midwest, I was overjoyed to arrive in Italy and meet our tour guide Santo—a total Italian stallion (and not in the Stallone way, more like a young Armand Assante). I had a feeling I was going to be get-ting more attention from Santo than the other women, since I was the only one in the group without an AARP card and bifocals—and I was right. The first night, after dinner, he asked me if I would like to take a boat ride in the Venice canals. "Yes, please," I responded, to which he replied in his hot Italian accent, "My, what a polite girl you are."*

*We ended up in his hotel room that night and every night after. He was amazing and so skilled I don't think anyone I've ever been with*

**THE BOYS' CLUB SAYS . . .**

Foreigners are awesome because they are better at sex than Americans. Every time—every single time. Of course, American women say the same thing about foreign men, so I guess we should all be heading over-seas.

—Bob, thirty-nine, Miami

*has surpassed him in bed. He spent hours making sure I was completely satisfied. The sex was incredible. I also think part of the thrill was the sneaking around and keeping it a secret. We were convinced we had kept our affair from my parents. I left at the end of that week and never saw or spoke to Santo again.*

*Cut to last Thanksgiving when the subject of secrets came up. I was saying how I would never keep anything from my folks. My mother responded with, "Oh really, what about your little Italian boy?" When the shock and red glow wore off my face, I took a deep breath and said, "Well, Mom, he was anything but little!" She shot me a knowing smile, and I shot her the same one back.*

—Annabelle, thirty-two, Denver

---

## SEXPRESSIONS

---

**forn**, *n.*, pornography in any language other than that of the audience, particularly that which contains graphic sex with obvious overdubbing

e.g., "If you watch the lips of the 'actors' and 'actresses' in forn, you might actually learn how to say 'Oh God' and 'Right there' in many different languages."

## Internet Action

In this day and age, the percentage of people who have dated, not to mention slept with, someone they met online has pretty much skyrocketed. It's not nearly as taboo as, say, responding to someone's personal ad in the paper—but it's basically the same thing. Therefore, there are more than a few reasons why this particular way of meeting up for some mutual macking can be either wonderful or wonderfully awful. Your first order of business, if you actually join an Internet dating site, is making sure the guy has a photo posted. As Ruth, twenty-three, of Los Angeles, says, "Online dating is the crack cocaine of the new millennium. It's cheap, addictive, and, well, very addictive. But if you do choose to join a dating site, let me warn you: the men are surprisingly intelligent, well read, well written, and even funny, but if they haven't posted a photograph, there is probably a reason." That reason would be that he's been beaten with the ugly stick, as if you didn't know.

Next, if you've got a profile and photo posted yourself, you should probably steer clear of commenting on the fact that you're just looking for a casual good time. This tactic tends to bring the creepiest of the creepy out of the woodwork. Suddenly, you're getting spammed by every loser from here to Southeast Asia, and it can get damn annoying.

Finally, don't just get to know each other via email. After the exchange of a few messages, in which you should actually steer clear of too much, if any, discussion of casual sex, arrange a time to chat on the phone. That's when, if he sounds reasonably articulate and normal, you can arrange to meet up in a safe, public place. If, when you do meet up, there is any physical chemistry (bear in mind this happens about once in every ten or twenty dates, max), invite him on over for a bottle of wine and have your way with him. Boom, you just pointed and clicked your way to some casual coitus. Nice one. (Just be aware that there's still a chance things could get sketchy—see chapter 8's "Nightmare Dot Com" Sexcapade from Saffron, thirty-five, of Hollywood, for example.)

| Ups | Downs |
|---|---|
| He can woo you with his fabulous wit and writing style. | When you get the visual, you realize all he's got going on is the wit and writing style. |
| He's just a mouse click away. | A mouse might be a better lay. |
| There are so many fish in the Internet sea. | The real catch could be that he's a serial killer. |

---

SEXPRESSIONS

---

**ASL (or asl)**, *n.*, stands for "Age, Sex, Location" and is typically used as a question when initiating a conversation in an Internet chat room (but is rarely answered truthfully)

e.g., John: "Hi, wanna cyber?" Jane: "ASL?" John: "28, male, San Francisco—and looking for a smart, sensitive, funny woman."

## Wedding Balls

If you're under the age of thirty or so, attending the nuptials of friends and loved ones can often present an ideal opportunity to hook up with a hottie. Once you get into your thirties and beyond, though, the pickings get slimmer and slimmer—and we're not talking about the guy's weight. Suddenly you're stuck at the singles' table with a few twelve-year-olds, the aunt of the groom whose husband just died, and the one or two geeky friends of the happy couple who desperately want to get married but haven't found the right person yet.

This is the only time when it might actually be a *good* thing to be a bridesmaid. Yes, we'll explain that one. Aside from the god-awful dress you may have to wear, at least you'll get to sit at the bridal party table, paired up with one of the groomsmen. If any of those groomsmen happen to be hot and single, then you've got a good shot at scoring some casual sex. See? Not all weddings suck. The only thing to keep in mind is whether or not there's a post-wedding brunch. And, of course, you should try your best to stay relatively sober. Otherwise, may the wedding night be rockin'.

| Ups | Downs |
| --- | --- |
| He gets to see you out of that pink taffeta dress you were forced to wear. | You'll have to put that damn dress back on when the deed is done. |
| Love is always in the air at a wedding. | Love is not what you want in the air after you've done him. |
| He's most likely a friend of a friend or a friend of the family. | Do you want your friends and family to get the full report on your actions? |

## SEXCAPADE: Going to the Chapel of Lust

*Last summer, I was asked to be in the wedding of a friend whom I rarely speak to. She was someone I grew up with, and I really didn't feel like dealing with the whole thing—from buying the bridesmaid dress to having to stand up in front of a bunch of people I had no interest in ever seeing again. But, I didn't really know how to say no, so I just went with it and hoped for the best.*

*A few days before the wedding, I headed out to California to deal with the prenuptial dinner and rehearsal stuff. The*

*bride-to-be introduced me to the rest of the wedding party, and*
*I was pleasantly surprised to meet Bart—the very cute grooms-*
*man with whom I'd be walking down the aisle. My friend later*
*pulled me aside and told me that she really didn't like Bart and*
*warned me to stay away from him. She said he was a player*
*who was always jumping from one girl to the next without ever*
*making a commitment to anyone. So, of course, I couldn't wait*
*to see what might transpire!*

*Bart and I got along incredibly well, and that night, we*
*decided to head to Las Vegas for some fun. We drove through*
*the night—stopping once in a while for some quickies in the car.*
*We indulged and played for the next couple of days, mostly in*
*the hotel room. Almost forgetting about the wedding, we drove*
*back on Sunday morning. We arrived in L.A. with about two*
*hours to spare. Needless to say, my friend was pissed (but I felt*
*too good to mind). The bride and groom have since divorced.*

—Julie, thirty-one, Long Island, New York

# The Competition-Free Man-Finder

If none of the scenarios we've described in this chapter have led to
you meeting more guys than you ever thought possible—if you're
not beating them off with a stick as much as you like to be—then we
offer this extra special look at the manliest locations ever. Of course,
you'll have to enter at your own risk. Just because there are a lot
more men than women there, that doesn't mean you'll want to do
them. See chapter 5 before you make that call.

- **Barber Shops.** Everyone needs a haircut sometime, right?

- **Batting Cages.** These guys know how to handle their bats—and their balls. Maybe you could teach them a trick or two, though.

- **Campgrounds.** So they may be smelly and dirty . . . but at least there's a campfire, plenty of beer, and perhaps a tent just big enough for two.

- **Comic Book Conventions.** Yes, most of the guys will be dorks. But probably dorks who haven't been laid in months, if not a lifetime. Sometimes a virgin sacrifice provides great entertainment value.

- **Dick-Flicks.** As in, action-adventure movies. No, you don't actually have to go and watch them. Just ask the kid at the ticket window what time it gets out ('cause you've gotta pick up your little brother); then seek out your get-off guy (and hope he's older than your little brother).

- **Firehouses.** What could be hotter than a fireman? Maybe he'll let you slide down his pole. Just ask him when he gets off.

- **Golf Courses.** Be smart and show up without the silly-looking outfits women who golf tend to wear, and you'll be any man on the links' hole in one.

- **Science or Mathematics Classes at the Local College.** Give those poor geeks a reason to get their heads out of the books, would you? Sometimes, brains-over-brawn makes for a far better bonk-fest, anyway.

- **Shooting Ranges.** If you're into redneck, right-wing, gun-toting types, then you'll be sure to find a man packing heat here.

- **Sporting Events.** There aren't just lots of balls on the court or field. They're in the stands too, and they come in pairs. If you like jocks, there will be plenty to get into here.

- **Sports Bars.** It's like going to a real bar, except no chick in her right mind would want to go unless she needs to get some, and fast.

- **Strip Clubs.** Why not? Everyone knows the guys are going to be hornier than hell—and you might get turned on in the process as well. He'll think it's cute that you're into the scene. Just keep in mind: you're meeting these guys at a strip club. Your call. 'Nuff said.

---

### SEXPRESSIONS

**frodosexual,** *n.*, a woman who enjoys having sex with geeks, particularly dorky guys who can't get enough of the *Lord of the Rings* trilogy

e.g., "Hanging out at dick-flicks is a great way to meet guys—but only if you're a frodosexual."

Now, riddle us this: Do you *really* believe that all the good ones (or at least the ones you can sleep with) are gay or taken, that you don't know anyone who can hook you up with a fine man for one hot night—or that guys who will give you a little action just don't hang out in the places you frequent? Well, maybe so, but as we've shown you, you've just got to be a little resourceful. So get out there and get some already, would you?

*Don't Do That Guy!*

*How to Spot and Ditch*

*the Losers*

# Chapter Five

# Date-Stoppers

ust because there are a lot of options out there, and just because you're horny, it's still not a given that you'll sleep with any guy who happens to come along—right? This is one of the biggest misconceptions about women who hook up: We're sluts, we're easy, we're whores or skanks or hos. Whatever label they put on you, it's imperative that you prove to the masses that you're not easy—that is, even if you're horny, not just any man will do (at least, he won't be doing you).

If you *will* sleep with any guy who comes along, you might want to do a little in-depth self-analysis. Seriously, a woman who will sleep with absolutely anyone might need to a) lighten up on the inebriating substances, or b) get paid for her services. Please don't misunderstand us—we make no judgment calls here. If you want to sleep with anyone and everyone, we really think it would be in your best interests to be profiting from it. You have the ability to do any man, to find something redeeming and worthwhile in even the lowest of the low, and for that, the oldest profession in the world could be yours—that or a gig in porn. Perhaps you could teach us a thing or two.

But we digress. If you are at least a little bit selective about who you'll sleep with, as noted in chapter 1, we urge you to rethink the terms society has forced upon you. You are not a slut, you are not a whore. Nay, dear woman, you are Slutalicious with a capital S. You get action because you deserve it and because you go for it. You call the shots; you tell him that his ass is yours. But the lucky guy who gets to do the nasty with you is going to have to prove he's worthy first—unlike our little friend Mike:

## SEXCAPADE: Midori Mike

*I was once set up on a blind date by a friend who assured me the guy was "really cute and really cool" and I would not be disappointed. I definitely saw potential when I arrived at my local neighborhood dive bar: Tall enough, nice hands, good hair, friendly eyes, tasteful shirt. All signs pointed to go. I sat down next to him at the bar and ordered my usual, Absolut martini, straight up, then looked at Mike. His next two words sealed his fate: "Midori sour." I was stunned. What was he thinking, ordering a girl drink with a bright smile and no irony? I downed my martini while coming up with my exit plan: "You know, I recently had food poisoning and I don't think it's quite gone—I never should have come out in the first place. I'm sorry," I said.*

*He understood, told me to feel better, and I got out of there as fast as I could. On the upside, I returned to the bar with my roommate the next Friday. When I ordered my usual, the hot bartender looked me straight in the eye, smiled, and said, "You sure you don't want a Midori sour?" I turned bright red, but he just laughed and gave me the most seductive look I've ever seen. Two hours later, I wound up at the bartender's house. He had beer in his fridge, a bottle of Jack on the counter—and I had a good time. A very good time. I hate to say it, but it doesn't hurt to pick (and ditch) your men by the beverages they consume.*

—Tracy, twenty-three, Atlanta

Behold, the plight of the single woman—or should we say "plights"? When it comes to men, there are more than a few Midori Mikes we'll be forced to endure. Okay, so bad taste in beverages may not be the biggest strike against a guy, but in this particular case, Tracy felt it was probably telling of other shortcomings Mike might eventually exhibit. As she told us, "When a guy looks or acts a certain way in one situation, you've got to figure it will translate into other behaviors, too. When Mike ordered that drink, my feeling was that he wasn't going to be able to deliver in the bedroom, and I'm the kind of girl who likes to cut her losses. I wanted action, but not that badly."

Yes, much as you may be looking to get it on, sometimes what's going to keep you from closing the deal—or even approaching it—is entirely in the hands of Mr. Man. Trust us when we say that there is no way you should dismiss the glaring, garish, grotesque guy-isms that run the gamut from personal hygiene to social or, horror of horrors, sexual disgraces. We'd like to say that some of these things can be worked on—that if you really knew the guy, they wouldn't be a big deal—but you know the drill: this isn't about finding Mr. Right, just Mr. Tonight. You don't have time to polish that diamond-in-the-rough.

# First Impressions: Things to Avoid at All Costs

The good news is that there are a lot of things a guy will do or say, from dressing or smelling a certain way to divulging some preliminary details about himself, that should promptly send you running for the hills. So pay close attention and consider yourself *very* lucky if you witness a warning sign before things have progressed too far, as Tracy did. The more information you gather about him early on, the more equipped you'll be to gauge (and avoid) what might later manifest in the bedroom. Of course, there are a million ways a guy can make a first impression—if he passes all of these tests, you may be okay. But you may not. Stay tuned after these first impressions for a shorter list of second impressions as well . . . you may still need to ditch the deed down the line.

## His Appearance and Hygiene

Certain style and sanitation practices need to come with a man, no matter how much time you plan on spending with him. If it looks like mommy's still dressing him, such fashion faux pas can tell you a lot about what he'll be like when he's *undressed* as well. And if you can smell him from a mile away now, that does not bode well for what's to come. We're talking potential STDs here, ladies, among many other atrocities. What follows are some of the most telling fashion and odor emergencies.

### STYLE (OR LACK THEREOF)

- flip-flops with socks
- Birkenstocks with socks
- any sandals with socks
- loafers
- shoes with tassels
- shorts with tube socks

- white jeans
- tight jeans
- tight white jeans
- bike shorts
- tight spandex anything
- acid-washed anything
- camouflage anything
- tie-dyed anything
- Hawaiian shirts (unless he's actually Hawaiian)
- T-shirts with slogans ("Coed Naked Lacrosse"; "Only cream and bastards rise to the top")
- visors and headbands
- T-shirts with animated characters (The Simpsons; Disney characters; *South Park* characters)
- rainbow suspenders
- funny ties (that are only funny to him)
- muscle shirts
- mesh tank tops
- Speedos
- wedding bands
- Guido medallions
- pinky rings
- skirts

## HAIR

- mullets (also known as "the bi-level"; "hockey hair"; "business in the front, party in the back"; "Kentucky waterfall"; "neck warmer"; "neck blankey"; "Camaro cut"; "Canadian passport")
- comb-overs
- toupees
- hair plugs
- high-and-tights/crew cuts
- ponytails
- long hair
- bozo hair (long on sides, bald on top)
- excessive use of hair products
- dandruff
- extreme grease

- bad teeth (the "Bubba" over-bite; blackened; extremely yellow; missing)
- visible nose hairs
- a monobrow/unibrow
- multiple ear piercings (more than two in each ear)
- overly groomed facial hair (see the Backstreet Boys)
- nips and tucks gone wrong (think: Kenny Rogers, Michael Jackson)

- extreme muscles
- fresh-from-the-tanning-bed bronze
- profuse sweating
- tattoos from head to toe
- an unnaturally large bulge

- vomit breath
- cigarette breath
- garlic breath
- stale breath
- body odor
- extreme cologne

## His Body Language and Basic Behavior

Ah, some guys and the things they do. More often than not, these juvenile male actions just smack of that "Please look at me *now*!" desperation—not something that sheds a positive light on the amount of attention he'll be paying to you in the bedroom. So don't let the following pleas for attention win yours.

- ass grabbing (yours or his)
- winking
- twitching
- spitting
- nose picking
- teeth picking
- giggling
- narcissism (checking himself out in the mirror)
- eye-wandering (checking out other girls)
- genitalia scratching
- adjusting of "the boys"
- continual voice-mail checking/cell-phone talking
- limp handshaking
- back patting

- air-guitar playing
- air drumming
- head banging
- dancing (too well or too poorly)
- drug pushing or taking (beware the nose that never stops running)
- overtly hitting on you
- not taking no for an answer
- trying to discreetly touch your breast (he'll call it a "boob") or your leg
- attempting to seductively whisper in your ear (he'll claim it's because it's "so loud in there"—even if it's quiet as a tomb)

## His Occupation

So, who cares what he does for a living, if you're not in it for the long haul? Well, you might not, for the most part—unless, that is, his profession translates to some other personality quirks you just don't want to deal with. If he actually admits to doing any of these things for a living, send him on a permanent vacation, without play. Also note that a lot of men lie about what they do, so have your bullshit detector on at all times.

- porn star
- model
- policeman
- postal worker

- politician
- priest
- male prostitute
- drug dealer

## The Heavy Hitter

A note of caution when you're out cruising for some casual coitus: beware of the men who hit on you, who buy you drinks, who caress you and tell you how beautiful you are, or generally just lay it on thick. Even look out for cheesy little ways he may try to steal you away from your friends or get you to go off somewhere together right away. Yes, you are attempting to score sex yourself—but the key here is to make sure you're the one in charge, not him. Never let a guy pick you up unless you're the one who approached him or unless he seems like someone you would have picked out yourself. Otherwise, you're being had—and you really need to make sure it's completely mutual at all times. Just don't let yourself be manipulated into doing anything you may not want to do with this particular person.

## SEXPRESSIONS

**viaggravate,** *v.*, when a male hits on a younger woman excessively, to the point where she fears he may actually begin humping her leg at any moment

e.g., "Ewww, scary grandpa man is fully viaggravating me. Let's go."

**fawnication,** *n.*, the act of fawning all over someone in order to get sex. Also see "fauxmantic."

e.g., "He wooed her with fawnication, including buying her drinks, rubbing her neck, and telling her how beautiful she was—but he laid it on so thick, he didn't get laid."

**fauxmantic,** *adj.*, pretending to have feelings of love in order to get laid or (*n.*) the act thereof

e.g., "Gregg took me to dinner and the movies last night—but when he insisted on a nightcap on his penthouse patio, claiming that my 'hair was shimmering in the moonlight,' I knew he was just getting fauxmantic."

## His Background or Lifestyle

What's done is done, and you just want to do him—or do you? When it comes to a guy's past (and possibly his present), always err on the side of caution. Some of these skeletons in the closet aren't worth sleeping with. Do a little background check before you take it to the bedroom, and if any of these qualities are part of the package, you'll want to lose this luggage.

**LIFESTYLES TO LOSE**

- frat boys
- ex-cons
- drug users
- any kind of addicts
- married men
- rednecks
- racists
- nudists
- swingers

## Sᴇxᴄᴀᴘᴀᴅᴇ: She Has Her Limits

*There are a number of things that will stop me from sleeping with someone: if they're a bigot or racist; if they smell bad or have on too much cologne; if they are uptight about sex and won't do certain things or are grossed out by things. On the other hand, I'm embarrassed to admit that I gave a Republican a blow job while he was driving me home from our first date. If Republican doesn't stop me, I guess not much will.*
    —Marsha, thirty-five, Saratoga, New York

## His Wheels

A lot of men believe that their vehicle is an extension of their penis. Given this, it makes sense that certain automobiles immediately translate into a casual sex stoplight, as they may indicate he's lacking down below, incapable of getting it up, or that he has some other odd bedroom behavior you're *not* going to want to touch. So if he pulls up in one of these, peel out of there.

### VEHICLES TO AVOID

- Camaro/Trans Am
- T-Bird
- El Camino
- Corvette
- Lamborghini
- Ferrari
- Hummer

- Sport bike (also known as a "crotch rocket")
- anything with a car bra
- anything with sheepskin seat covers
- a bicycle
- a skateboard

## His Vocabulary

Public speaking is a fear worse than death for most people, and encountering any of these speaking patterns in public should make you realize sex with this guy will be a *fate* worse than death. Translation? No habla el sex for these guys. Give him a vocab test, and if any of the following are used—well, he fails.

### EXPRESSIONS TO AVOID

- "I want to pork you."
- "You wanna bang?"
- "babe"
- "bro"
- "pussy"
- "bitch"
- "whore"
- "ho"
- "slut"
- "broad"
- "rack"
- "boobs"

- "cunt" (unless you're in the U.K., where this is actually a cute little slang term—just make sure it's not directed at you)
- excessive mentions of other girls he's dated/done
- he refers to himself in the third person (for instance, "Jeff is really liking you, babe!"—now that's what we call a double whammy)
- he uses a cheesy pickup line (yes, "you're so beautiful" qualifies)

## His Sexual Orientation

This may seem obvious to most, but sometimes even a guy doesn't realize that he really wants to do other guys. He may not be aware of it yet, but you should be. You know the type: he's a girl's best friend—and that's as far as it goes. So don't deny it. He's just not going to go there, girlfriend. Make him your shopping buddy instead, because if any of these signs are there, you're not going to be getting any, anyway.

- better shoes or clothes than yours
- mesh tank tops
- satin clothing
- velvet clothing
- leather clothing (questionable)
- pink or leopard-print anything (clothes, home décor)
- lots of antiques in the home
- big, poofy beds
- highlighted/extremely frosted hair
- semen breath
- uncontrollably giggly
- incredible dancer
- stripper/exotic dancer; priest
- Miata or Volkswagen Cabriolet driver
- satin sheets
- white lacquer furniture
- canopy bed
- poodle owner
- gayisms ("You go, girl!"; "dreamy!")
- girly drinker (Midori sour; flavored malt beverages; wine coolers; light beer; fruity drinks with umbrellas; fruit-flavored martinis; anything pink; anything creamy)
- body piercings (navel, nipple, and tongue rings may be questionable—consider the context and proceed with caution)
- ear cuffs
- vast knowledge of musical theater
- fan of Madonna, Cher, Judy Garland, Bette Midler, and/or techno music

## SEXPRESSIONS

**metrosexual,** *n.*, also known as "fauxmosexual," *n.* a guy who likes to take care of himself—expensive clothes and shoes, well groomed, well read, well spoken. Some also call him a gay-acting straight guy.

e.g., "When I went to the salon last week, there were two metrosexuals waiting to get facials."

**manscape,** *v.*, the male metrosexual act of removing body hair from the face, arms, chest, back, legs, pubic area, to enhance appearance

e.g., "Too bad the guy I met at Giovanni's last night wasn't familiar with the concept of manscaping, which I should have known from the tufts of hair bursting from his collar."

**Jethrosexual,** *n.*, a manly heterosexual of the redneck variety; the opposite of metrosexual

e.g., "Bart drives a truck, drinks Budweiser, and has never used a hygiene product in his life. Yes, he's a Jethrosexual."

### THE BOYS' CLUB SAYS . . .

I was at a friend's art gallery opening and I noticed that most everyone, male or female, had a martini glass filled with a bright pink drink that had been topped off with some dry ice for this wild steaming effect. While I was curious and tempted to get one, by the time I got to the bar, I spotted this really hot woman in the corner of the room alone. I imagined what she would think if I approached her with a pink cocktail in hand and then promptly ordered a Remy neat.

—*Virgil, twenty-nine, Hollywood*

## His Kissing Style

If you don't know what qualifies as a bad kisser, you probably shouldn't be going any further until you figure that out. After all, kissing is a preview of what's to come (so to speak). Therefore, study our make-out meter, and consider going no further if any of the following techniques are being used.

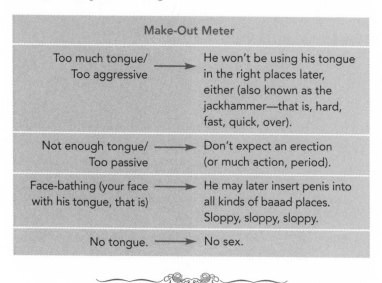

| Make-Out Meter | |
| --- | --- |
| Too much tongue/ Too aggressive → | He won't be using his tongue in the right places later, either (also known as the jackhammer—that is, hard, fast, quick, over). |
| Not enough tongue/ Too passive → | Don't expect an erection (or much action, period). |
| Face-bathing (your face with his tongue, that is) → | He may later insert penis into all kinds of baaad places. Sloppy, sloppy, sloppy. |
| No tongue. → | No sex. |

### SEXCAPADE: Shooting Darts

*I was at a party, and this guy and I went into the bathroom to make out, which I hoped would lead to other fun acts. When he was kissing me, I kept thinking, I'm not your mother—can't you do more than just peck-peck-peck at me? Do you not have a tongue?*

—Connie, thirty-five, Toronto

# Second Impressions: When the Clothes Come Off

If you've made it this far and he's avoided exhibiting any of the afore-mentioned date-stoppers, congratulations! You may have yourself a man for the night. But beware: the deal isn't done yet. There are still a few things he may do, even mid-deed, to send you running. Consider the story of Allison, for instance:

## SEXCAPADE: The Lil' Guy

*My friend Cathy and I went out one night to see a movie, then decided to go to a bar around the corner. On our way there, we ran into a guy Cathy really liked, and she asked him to join us. We all headed to the bar together, where the guy called his room-mate to join us (maybe he thought we'd hit it off or something).*

*When the roommate showed up, I was not impressed: he was beer-bellied and balding, and I was hoping that Cathy and I could take off when the bar closed. No such luck. The guy and his roommate invited us over to their place, and Cathy managed to convince me to go with them.*

*Back at their place, Cathy and the object of her desire disap-peared, and there I was with beer-bellied bald guy, on the couch, making small talk. The topic headed in a sexual direction, and we began talking about our worst experiences ever. I revealed that the first guy I ever slept with had a tiny penis, at which point "baldy" decided to tell me that his penis was tiny, too. Then he asked if I wanted to see it—like I needed proof. I said no, but he showed me anyway. For a second, I thought he was doing some sort of magic trick with his thumb—that was about the size of it.*

*I'm not exactly sure what happened next, but somehow he convinced me to follow him to his bedroom. Temporary insanity or a few too many drinks, I guess. Things just got worse from there, primarily because the poor guy couldn't get it up. So, not only was it only an inch or two long, but it was limp. He told me to put my head down there and suckle it like a nipple. After trying for about twenty minutes to get him aroused (why, oh why, did I even try?), I just gave up. I felt bad, but it wasn't going to be worth my effort, in any case, and the alcohol was wearing off fast.*

*So, I got up, put my clothes on, said, "Thanks anyway, but this obviously isn't working," and got out of there as fast as I could. Fortunately, I never saw that guy again—although, about a year later, he hit on Cathy at a party. She couldn't help but laugh when she remembered what I'd told her about the poor lil' guy.*

—Allison, twenty-nine, San Diego

---

### SEXPRESSIONS

**migitian**, *n.*, a guy who isn't well endowed (Best when said while holding up your pinky finger and wiggling it.)

e.g., "I was so disappointed when we finally got naked—turns out, he was a migitian."

---

So, you had too much to drink, didn't see the writing on the wall, or were simply too horny to opt against doing a guy you knew might not be worthy. It's happened to the best of us. But that doesn't mean you have to stick around, if the performance has started, but the show is boring you to tears or frightening beyond your worst fears. Do *not* be afraid to run for the door and ditch the deed, just when it's going down. There are things guys will do—especially when you don't really know them—that you just shouldn't be putting up with. What are these act 2 atrocities? Here are some of the biggies.

## His Place

Homeward bound? If the action winds up at his abode, you may learn a lot more about the guy—maybe too much. (See chapter 7 for more on this topic.) Many of the following domestic don'ts will make for one miserable walk of shame. So don't let your intentions for action overrule what you discover upon arrival. There's still time! Make your move . . . and we don't mean into his bedroom.

---

### HABITAT HORRORS

- lives with Mommy
- lives with twelve other guys
- Star Trek posters
- PlayStation as the center-piece of the living room
- posters with cute animals (e.g., kitty hanging from tree with the phrase "Hang in there!")
- posters or actual framed prints of muscle cars
- girlie calendars (particularly those with the Budweiser girls or the Barbi twins)
- stuffed animals in the bedroom
- wicker or rattan furniture

- wall-sized (or ceiling-sized) mirrors
- creepy, ostentatious (bedroom) furniture
- S&M equipment
- religious paraphernalia
- porno mags in the bathroom
- bad music on the stereo (e.g., John Tesh or Insane Clown Posse)
- a dirty and disgusting dump (hasn't cleaned in months, doesn't own a set of sheets, and you're scared to touch anything)
- the ultimate cheesy bachelor pad designed for seduction

**technosexual,** *n.*, a guy who would rather play video games than have sex

e.g., "I thought we were going to screw, but he turned out to be a technosexual and just stared at his Playstation all night."

## SEXCAPADE: Not So Super

*This guy came into my office and asked me to a modern jazz concert. I hate modern jazz—the only reason I said yes was a) I was young and b) he was hot. When I say hot, I mean he epitomized what every teenage girl's fantasy (or at least mine) probably was in the eighties: tall and blonde with big bangs like that guy in the Thompson Twins. I thought he was super smart. I think he went to Cornell. He may have been a gradu- ate student—I can't remember. Anyway, we went to the concert, and it was as awful as I had anticipated.*

*After the show, we went back to his place for a drink, and things got even cheesier. He had black leather sofas and love seats. It was a beautiful, spacious, rich-kid condo that his par- ents had clearly financed—but in an American Psycho kind of way. After a couple of drinks, we proceeded to have what I imag- ine he thought was "wild, crazy" sex—in the bathroom (I think he actually had a map-of-the-world shower curtain), on the sticky leather couch, and in his bedroom. I finally had to fake an orgasm, just so he would finish and I could leave. But I was so loud that his building super started knocking on the door, ask- ing if everything was okay. The cheesebag was on cloud nine. The punch line is that it was the worst sex I have ever had.*

—Amanda, thirty-two, Brooklyn

## Sexcapade: Ah, Sheet!

*I went home with this guy, we fooled around, and then I fell asleep for a while. I woke up and noticed that we were sleeping on California Raisins sheets. I left immediately."*
—Marni, thirty-four, Chicago

## His (Unclothed) Appearance and Hygiene

So it's got to that point. He's revealed himself. But there's still time to take off, after he's taken it off, if absolutely necessary—and if you discover any of these physical atrocities on the disrobed road … run, don't walk.

### BODY, SKIVVIES, AND SCENTS

- G-strings or women's underwear
- hairy backs or body rugs
- smooth all over (i.e., clean-shaven . . . everywhere)
- multiple body piercings (nipples *and* navel *and* 'nads? Oh my.)
- track marks
- profuse sweating
- body odor or extreme cologne (if you didn't catch a whiff until now)
- man-breasts (he needs a bra more than you do)
- a limp or little penis
- elephantitis of the genitalia
- excessive pubic shedding
- herpes
- open sores (do we need to tell you this?)

## SEXCAPADE: A Man Down Undie

*I had been hanging out with this cute Australian rock climber
who had recently moved to town. He was funny and cute, and
he adored me. One night, we had so much fun drinking at the
bar below my apartment and singing karaoke that we went
upstairs and listened to records. Yes, records.*

*We were kissing a bit and I was
considering more when he undressed
to his skivvies. He was wearing tight
leopard skin Speedo-type underwear.
I was totally thrown because he was
this outdoorsy, ruggedly handsome*
*sort of guy. I was so flustered and surprised by the underwear
that I really just wanted to laugh but didn't want to hurt his
feelings. Thus, I crawled into bed and quickly fell to sleep, or
so it seemed.*

*Later in the week after I had blown him off, he confronted
me while I waited in line to get inside the bar downstairs. He
loudly asked me why I didn't call him, and when I said I was
busy, he yelled, "But we slept together!"*
*I embarrassingly replied, "No, we didn't, and no we won't." In
literal terms, he was right—we slept* next *to* each *other. But in
reality, he was as unlucky as the leopard who gave his life for a
pair of boys' panties.*

—Adelle, thirty-five, Los Angeles

## His Sexual Behavior

There's a chance that the sex may not be the best you've ever had, but there are definite ways of ensuring you have a good time, instead of a bad one. Even if you're in the middle of getting it on, there are certain behaviors that no man should ever attempt with a girl, particularly when he doesn't know her that well. We all have our limits. "I hate when guys try to do that pouty sex face. I might not leave, but it would make me laugh," notes Diana, thirty-one, of Chicago. Meanwhile, Mary, thirty, of Houston, says, "I would stop having sex with a guy if he moaned or wailed louder than me during foreplay or intercourse." Don't worry about blue-balling him—if he pulls any of these maneuvers, he's probably used to indigo down below, anyway. In a nutshell: if any of the following transpire, reprimand him or, better yet, bail.

### SEX ACTS TO AVOID

- condom refusal (no glove? no love)
- he tells you to take a shower beforehand
- he breaks out the sex toys (you can break them out if you want to—he never should)
- he puts a porno in the VCR
- he tries to make a porno (that is, he busts out the camcorder)
- he attempts the fellate-me-now, pushing your head down move ("You're not Spielberg—don't direct me—I'll get there.")
- he refers to his genitals—or yours—by a name
- painful sex play (when the fine line between pleasure and pain is crossed)
- overly enthusiastic rubbing or spanking (unless you're into that kind of thing)

- "We're porn stars" maneuvers (the money shot, the facial)
- porno-speak/verbal demands or commands ("make noise!"; "faster!"; "harder!"; "louder!")
- disrespectful maneuvers (attempting to come in your mouth; going to the butt; requesting you give/receive a "golden shower")

- asking you to rim him or go to his butt
- "funky spunk" (if this isn't the final blow, so to speak, get out while you still can)

## SEXCAPADE: Boogie in the Butt

*I was sleeping with this guy Ken—we had about three booty calls over the course of a month, and he was really good in bed. I liked that he was respectful and always willing to please me. We were also comfortable enough with each other to be able to say what we wanted—which ultimately proved problematic.*

*In the middle of round four he told me he wanted me to stick my finger up his ass while I was going down on him. I didn't know what to do. Maybe some people are okay with doing that but not me. I told him that I just didn't feel comfortable going there, and he asked me to at least try it. He said it was a really big turn-on for him and many other men too. I figured I should try everything at least once, so I gave my index finger one last, long look and plunged it in.*

*I could see it was turning him on, but I've got to say it had the opposite effect on me. It took me hours of repeated hand*

*washing to get that stink off of me, and I promptly "lost" Ken's*
*number. Since then, I've asked a lot of my male friends and*
*sex partners if it was actually something they're into. Maybe*
*they're lying, but to this day, not one has admitted to the bum-*
*fingered blow job being a turn-on.*

—Mira, thirty-three, Long Island, New York

# Final Impressions: After the Fact

When all is said and done, some of us are simply so anxious to get
action that we just go with it, whether the date-stopping signs are
there or not. Don't dismay. The experience wasn't all for naught. You
did get laid, and that's something to celebrate—as well as something
that educates. So, what did you learn, good or bad? How will this
man and the things he did, particularly if they were wrong, help you
to make sure your next man is more of what you want? Here's what
Sherilynn took away from one conquest:

### SEXCAPADE: Check Your Panties Here

*I had been looking forward to going to see my friend's new*
*band for a really long time, but, unfortunately, when I finally*
*did, I wasn't really into it. The music was so boring that my*
*eyes began to wander—right over to a cute guy who'd just come*
*in. He had sort of an Ethan Hawke grunge thing going on,*
*with a flannel shirt and scruffy hair—exactly my type back in*
*the nineties. After we checked each other out for the better*
*part of a half hour, I motioned for him to come over. About an*
*hour later at my friend's house, we were on the tiny guest*

room couch, the cushions kept slipping down, and we didn't have a condom—it was all just bad, bad, bad.

The next morning, "Ethan" took off pretty early. I looked around, and we'd just about destroyed the couch. Plus we'd had unprotected sex. I had so many regrets, and then to add insult to injury, my friends filled me in on something I hadn't even noticed: the guy had been wearing a T-shirt under his flannel shirt that said, "Check your panties here." Well, I guess I'm pretty good at following directions—not that I'd actually seen them. Now I always carefully scrutinize a guy's clothes before hooking up with him.

—Sherilynn, twenty-six, San Francisco

Whether you saw the warning signs and stopped the sex from happening, you cut out in the middle, or you went all the way and had some regrets later on, most one-night stands can teach us a little something about ourselves, not to mention the need for putting some limits on our libidos. Sherilynn told us about several of her regrets but also said that she took away some valuable lessons. "I *never* go all the way without a condom anymore," she notes. "And I really am conscious of a guy's clothes, demeanor, everything. I know this might sound a little unlikely, but maybe if I'd seen what the guy's shirt said, I would have known he was a player who uses women a lot more than he uses condoms—or something."

So what are your strategies going to be the next time you meet a guy with "date-stopper" (or a stupid T-shirt slogan) written all over him? What are the best tactics for making a clean break as painlessly and quickly as possible? First of all, make sure you realize that this is no longer the time to play it cool or obsess about how you might look; quite the opposite, in fact. When you realize he's not right for tonight, you need to do whatever it takes to put some distance between you and him. Here are some of your best bets for doing so.

# The Last Word: Twenty Tips to Alienate the Date-Stoppers

1. **Say something offensive.** It's okay to come across as a raging bitch when you're trying to get rid of a guy. Try something like "Wow, there sure are a lot of ugly guys here tonight," "Why are all the hot men taken?" or "I can see why you're still single" to send him off and running.

2. **Say something whiny.** Be as annoying as possible, and you won't have to deal with the guy for long. Your tone of voice is key here, as is your facial expression (think: something smells really sour), and lines like "This music sucks," "I'm so bored," or "Ewww, this drink is terrible/warm/flat/not strong enough/too strong" should do the trick.

3. **Turn into a man-hater.** Say anything that might bruise the male ego or scare the crap out of him—again, be bitchy and you'll lose the boy fast. Talk about how your ex was such an asshole, how men are keeping women down in the workplace and society at large, or simply take a feminist stance on anything he happens to say.

4. **Be an opinionated, condescending know-it-all.** Any time he expresses his thoughts on something, play devil's advocate. "That's what *you* think" is a great way to start every sentence, followed by a dogmatic, narrow-minded statement on any range of topics, from what you think of the president to gun control to the state of world affairs.

5. Turn into a cult leader. Hard sell him on anything that might drive him away. For instance, start singing the praises of the Church of Scientology, or try to get him to invest in a pyramid scheme.

6. Ignore him. Don't make eye contact with him and flirt with any man in the vicinity other than the date-stopper (the bartender is always a good option), and he should get the picture pretty fast.

7. Be disgusting. If getting rid of him is proving particularly difficult, engage in any grotesque behavior, from picking your nose to belching to spitting (unless, of course, this is the same behavior the date-stopper is engaging in; then it might just endear you to him).

8. Talk periods. Many men cringe at the mere mention of menstruation. To really send him running for the hills, start by talking about how bad your cramps are, and take it as far as you need to from there.

9. Talk about yourself in the third person. As soon as you realize you're not into the guy, replace the word "I" with your name in every sentence. Saying things like "Amy has to go pee pee," "Amy is not amused by you," or "Amy thinks men who say such things are evil" should help to freak him out. (Again, avoid this tactic if this is the offensive behavior of the date-stopper himself.)

10. Find the Lord. Begin talking about how much your life has changed since you've found God/Christ/the Holy Spirit/Yahweh/Buddha/Allah; if he's not a religious guy himself, this should get him praying for your exit.

11. **Baby talk.** Turn into a five-year-old and begin pouting or coddling him. Scrunch your face up as you tell him he's just the cutest little puppy-puppy or that you have to go poopy-poopy.

12. **Lose your etiquette.** Forget about being prim and proper when the guy is a true date-stopper. Bum a cigarette (or light your own), making sure to blow smoke directly in his face, laugh like a hyena, drink your cocktail so enthusiastically that most of it dribbles down your face, or sneeze in his face, and he won't be sticking around for long.

13. **Sing it loud.** Start singing along to the jukebox in the worst possible voice—as loudly and as off-key as you can—to the point where listening to you is anything *but* music to his ears.

14. **Soil yourself.** Drop your drink in your lap, and run off to clean yourself up, never to return again.

15. **Groom him.** Begin picking at or brushing imaginary lint from his clothes, smooth his hair, and begin to list all of the ways that you could make him look better. He won't be around long enough to find out the rest of your plans.

16. **Go lesbo.** While girl-on-girl action turns a lot of guys on, if you pay enough attention to your girlfriend(s), to the exclusion of all men in the vicinity, the offensive date-stopper should eventually get the picture and leave.

17. **Become a hypochondriac.** Men don't exactly dig sick chicks, so try talking about how you think you've got mono, how you're sure you're going to get cancer any day now, how the world is so polluted that we're all going to die—and he'll make sure he doesn't catch any of what you've got going on.

18. Become a master impressionist. Do your best Austin Powers ("Do I make you horny?"), valley girl ("Totally!") or Terminator ("I'll be back")—and you'll be sure to leave a *bad* impression on him.

19. Play the creepy name game. Ask him what his last name is, then try out your first name with it, out loud, over and over and over again—as you slowly watch him walk away.

20. Forget him. As soon as you realize you want to get rid of the guy, call him any male name other than his.

Sad but true: not *every* guy is going to have it going on or be worth your time—even for one night of carnal pleasures. If that's the unfortunate case, you've now got plenty of tools at your disposal for hauling your ass on outta there. If you don't wind up extracting yourself until after the fact, well, at least consider yourself to be a little bit wiser, and ready to stop that date before it happens the next time.

*Yes, Men Are Easy.*

*Here's How to*

*Make Sure of It*

# Chapter Six

# Closing the Deal

Finally, we've got all the preliminaries out of the way, and it's time to ride that man off into the sunset. If you've found your one-night opportunity, and he hasn't done anything to send you running for the hills, then all that's left to do is make sure he's as interested in doing the deed as you are. When we polled women around the country to find out how they score themselves a guaranteed one-night stand, most of them laughed and said, "I just look in his general direction"—and while we all know that most guys are easy, that doesn't mean they all are (yes, really). Just as there are certain males who seriously repel us, as delineated in the previous chapter, believe it or not, some of us can, on rare occasions, repel them, too (and not just the ones who swing the other way, much as we'd like to think any man who doesn't want us *must* be gay).

We're not saying that women can be anywhere near as grotesque as a lot of guys—in fact, it's our feeling that most women are pretty good at tending to the basics required to attract a man. Even so, not all men are going to be hot for any and all women, whether we've done something wrong, look unappealing, or simply aren't their speed. We'd like to think of it as your good old run-of-the-mill absence of chemistry, and leave it at that. After all, we've been turned down a few times ourselves, and it wasn't always pretty. Thanks to our friend Candace, we know we're not alone (and neither are you):

## SEXCAPADE: Lights, Camera, No Action

*My worst casual sex experience? The one that never happened. After I tell you this story, you may find it hard to believe that I've slept with enough guys to know that I'm worth someone's while—but I've definitely been around the block a few times, and thought I was getting pretty good at it. In fact, on this particular night of rejection, I'd already had a final farewell fuck with my ex, as well as amazing sex with a friend of a friend, within the past week (within a day of each other, truth be told). I felt like I was on a roll—like I could get anyone—and I had my eye on one particular guy: a friend of my cousin's who was a screenwriter. He was really cute, I'd seen him at a few parties my cousin had had, and I really wanted to get to know him better.*

*I actually passed up going to a party where I was almost certain I could hook up with the aforementioned friend of a friend to go to this other party and chat up my cousin's friend. So, I go to this party and I have my eye on screenwriter guy all night. We have a few moments here and there where I think he might be into me. I get drunk enough to muster my courage and, finally, I sit down on the floor in the living room, he looks down at me, and I gesture to him to join me.*

*"How's it going?" I ask. He seems a little uncomfortable, but clearly is trying to go with it, and manages an "Uh, okay."*

So, I look into his eyes, trying to figure out if he's interested or not. Unable to get a clear read, I decide to throw caution to the wind and go for it anyway. "You know," I say, trying to be as cool and non-drunk as possible, "the only reason I came here tonight was because I was hoping you'd be here."

Silence. The poor guy looked like he was about to crap in his pants. "Um . . . yeah . . . I mean, I saw you at my cousin's last party, but we never got to talk—and I really wanted to get to know you better," I said.

Silence again. Seriously, this guy who has penned movie scripts had absolutely no lines in him—not even a "thanks, but I'm not interested." Needless to say, I was not his type. So sometimes I'm just not a good judge of character—certainly in this scenario, anyway. A few moments later, with still nary a reply, I opted to cut my losses and salvage what little pride I had left. So, I stood up and said, "Okay, well, there it is . . . have a good night"—found my cousin, and took off.

I felt completely rejected, like some sort of leper. But you know what? I let it bum me out for about twenty-four hours. The next day, I sent an email to the sad little screenwriter letting him know that he shouldn't have taken the fact that I hit on him too much to heart since I develop crushes on most of my cousin's male friends pretty easily. It was funny, not too harsh—just enough to make sure I hadn't scared him completely, so future crossings-of-paths wouldn't be too awkward. Still no response—but no biggie, I decided. At least I tried. And so it goes . . .

Ultimately, I guess it was a good thing he didn't respond (on all occasions). It allowed me to see his true colors—what I like to call the shades of an invertebrate! More than that, though, I saw that he wasn't interested in me. So, I lost that *particular game . . . but a week later, I was back in the saddle with someone who was interested (and much better with a comeback). No harm, no foul.*

—Candace, thirty-four, Sherman Oaks, California

The bottom line: female or not, you won't be able score every time. There's the rub. Certain situations simply can't be controlled, particularly when more than one person is involved. Candace made reference to the fact that the screenwriter was a little spineless, which is valid enough. But she also acknowledged that the key reason for the rejection was that the guy just wasn't into her. Is that such a bad thing? Of course not.

Maybe it has something to do with the guy's shortcomings, but whatever the situation, if the two of you aren't going to work, you've basically just got to accept it. 'Nuff said. Given this, before we go over the ways to ensure you'll score that guy you've been eyeing, let's go over your worst-case scenarios and how to handle them gracefully.

# Desperate, but Not Serious

Our experiences have taught us that it's the guys you can't get into bed whom you're probably going to want most of all. The more elusive he is, the hotter he becomes. But regardless of who he is or what he looks like, rejection stings and it could possibly sting you. If you find yourself in that unfortunate situation, it's natural to let every defense mechanism you've ever experienced come up. However, it's not only going to wind up making you look worse—it may make you look, horror of horrors, *desperate*.

As we're sure you know, the desperate girl is a total turnoff. She may think she's being a ball-busting bundle of confidence when she starts spouting off about what a loser the guy who's just rejected her is. Unfortunately, at that point, she's anything but self-assured. We don't want to sound like "rules girls" here—that's pathetically dishonest—but if you pay attention to these suggestions, getting turned down might actually wind up being a blessing in disguise.

## The Rules of Rejection

How should you go for the guy—and how should you react when he doesn't want you as much as you want him? Here we go:

- Do pick one guy you'd like to take home and concentrate on closing him.

- Don't get a little (or a lot) tipsy and throw yourself on any guy with a pulse (hot or not).

- Do be confident and go for what you want in a straightforward manner.

- Don't let your desperation for the guy show.

- Do take the advice of our beloved Kenny Rogers and know when to fold 'em, walk away, and run.

- Don't beat a dead horse and lose your dignity—especially when the guy who's actually worth your while might just be three stools down the bar.

- Do cut your losses and bow out gracefully.

- Don't start coming up with all the reasons why he's a loser for not wanting to do you.

- Do believe that it's not your loss—it's his.

- Don't let the situation affect how you feel about yourself. You've got it going on, he just can't see it.

**THE BOYS' CLUB SAYS . . .**

I went to a wedding last year where I was seated at the singles table with a very attractive girl sitting across from me. Eventually, we wound up next to each other, but she wasn't very bright, and the conversation deteriorated with each gin and tonic she knocked back. Finally, at the end of the evening, as we were waiting for our cars, she told me that there were a million different men who were dying to fuck her, and that—lucky me—she'd decided she would go home with me. She was completely slurring and embarrassing herself. I politely declined, at which point she screamed at the top of her lungs, "Oh, I get it—you're gay!" I would have felt sorry for myself, but I was too busy feeling sorry for her. I just got in my car and drove off.

—*Marcus, forty-two, Olympia, Washington*

### SEXCAPADE: Fill 'Er Up (Not)

*I was on my way home with a guy one night, and we stopped at a gas station to buy condoms. He asked me to go inside and get them (duh—I'm the asshole that did). By the time I got back outside, he was gone.*

—Jenny, thirty-two, Santa Cruz, California

Now that we've accepted the brutal reality that rejection is a possibility, let's venture on over to the better-case scenario: increasing your odds for some serious action. While no plan absolutely guarantees you'll get the guy you want, we've certainly learned a few tricks through the years, and so have plenty of other women. How can you get that big, hot stud into bed? Let us count the ways . . .

# Step 1: Aphrodisiacs

Sure, some people say it's a crock, but we think it's pretty fascinating that foods might be your secret weapon for getting someone in the sack. In fact, we're feeling a little excited just thinking about it! So if you find yourself in the general vicinity of a restaurant, kitchen, or another place where edibles are readily available, we'd venture to guess it might be worthwhile for you to brush up on some of the finer points of foods that get you (and the men) going. Although Dr. Ava told us "aphrodisiacs are rarely necessary when both people are generally ready, willing, and able to have casual sex," our feeling is you may as well stack the deck in your favor as much as possible.

In fact, there are actual doctors—medical doctors, no less—who have devoted their careers to doing research on how scents can be incredibly powerful in their ability to affect human behavior. Some such odors can serve as aphrodisiacs and send the blood southward (yes, we mean to the genitals—and no, we're not talking about Aunt Flow). Specifically, Alan R. Hirsch, neurological director of the Smell and Taste Treatment and Research Foundation in Chicago, conducted a fairly comprehensive study on what scents spark sexual arousal. Not surprisingly, he told us that every last one he tested triggered a sexual response in men, although some were more powerful than others. Among his findings:

- The combined scent of lavender and pumpkin pie increased penile blood flow by 40 percent.

- The scent of buttered popcorn increased penile blood flow by 9 percent.

- The scent of cheese pizza increased penile blood flow by 5 percent.

- The scent of floral perfume increased penile blood flow by 3 percent.

We're talking about male arousal here, ladies—how to not just make him horny but get it up. Based on this, while we wouldn't necessarily guarantee it to work, why not try spritzing a little lavender on yourself and your bedding before you go out—or, better yet, do that and then invite that guy you've been hoping to get down with to the family Thanksgiving gathering? Hmmm. Okay, probably a long shot.

For what it's worth, there are also scents that can get the girls going—so if you're not in the mood but wish you were, check out these findings from Hirsch's study:

- The combination of licorice-flavored Good & Plenty and cucumber was the most potent sexual scent in increasing blood flow to the vaginal area.

- The combined scent of lavender and pumpkin pie also increased blood flow to the vagina.

- The scent of men's cologne actually lowered blood flow to the vagina, as did cherries and the odor of barbecue or roasting meat.

Obviously, a lot of these responses depend on the individual and are often based on your past experiences, as Hirsch confirmed to us. But there's no reason you shouldn't play with your food and different smells and see what works for you, right? After all, we know of at least one woman who discovered the way to a man's libido through the lab-tested scent of lavender:

## SEXCAPADE: Flower Power

*I love lavender. I mean I'm crazy for it. It's my favorite scent in the world. All the candles, bath products, moisturizers, shampoos, oils, and perfumes I own are lavender based. I also have a ritual I do: when I bring a guy home for some action, I always light a bunch of candles and spray my bed with lavender pillow and room spray. The response I get is truly amazing. Men really love it. Almost all have commented on the fragrance and said that my bed and my room were so comfortable and they love the way it smells. I don't know if it's helped to turn them on, but I do know nobody's complained yet!*

—Nancy, thirty-eight, Keithville, Louisiana

---

### SEXPRESSIONS

---

**afrodisiac**, *n.*, not to be confused with aphrodisiac, this is a hot, sexy black man (afro optional)

e.g., "Damn, girl, check out the afrodisiac walking this way."

# Step 2: Communication

Beyond exploring culinary delights that could spark casual coitus, one thing's for sure: if you don't let a man know what you want, you won't get it—but if you do, you improve your chances dramatically (sure, it didn't work for Candace, but at least she gave it her best shot). Look, females have been pigeonholed as being great communicators, so why not use that generalization to your advantage and start (or keep) talking? As Dr. Ava told us, "The best way to let a man know that you want to have casual sex is to talk about it. You can say that it has always been a fantasy of yours to have a handsome lover with no strings attached." While we're not advocating that you use those exact words, you can come up with your own way of letting him know what you want.

Dr. Ava suggests that the kinkier you make the conversation, the better (at least, that's what we think she meant): "Erotic conversation is a must. Tell him what you want him to do to you and let him know what you are going to do to him, in graphic detail." All right then, consider this a challenge: How dirty can you talk, and what's appropriate, when? If you're not sure how to get things going, you can always try out a pickup line—but as we all know, those rarely work, especially for men. When we polled men and women, asking for any surefire pickup lines they rely on to get someone into bed, most of them feigned horror and said, "Do people still use those?" Damn. We were hoping for a few. In the defense of a good pickup line, though, we will say that when placed in the right context, with attention to timing, and when delivered by a woman, they can get you exactly what you want in a matter of minutes. Here's one such example of just that:

## Sexcapade: **Check Your Head**

*One night, I went out to see a band, and a guy I worked with introduced me to his friend, John. I was there with a girlfriend, and I was impressed with the way John made sure to give his attention to both of us, so neither one felt ignored. He was clearly skilled in making girls feel good about themselves. After a few minutes, he asked us where our boyfriends or husbands were, and we both responded that we were single. I know he was being kind of a cheesebag with his leading question in the first place, and he was way over the top when he came back with, "How is that possible? That's such a crime that two hot girls like you would be single." But I bought it. I think I actually jumped up and down as I said, "I love you, John! No guy in this town has called me hot in at least a week!"*

*It was all just harmless flirtation, and it was fun. Then, my friend turned to me and reminded me that we had another show to go to, so we told John we were going to have to take off. "What?" he said. "You can't leave now. We're just getting to know each other." But, we were meeting friends at the other place and we didn't want to stand them up (actually, at this point I did, but I felt bad). John said he would go to the other club and let our friends know we weren't going to make it. He was laying it on so thick—and I was enjoying it.*

*I said, "Look, we really have to go . . . maybe we can all hang out another time." He said, "Okay, we better," and handed me his card. I looked at the card and said, "Um, you really want me to call you? Are you sure that's not going to freak you out?" And he said, "No, in fact, I'll be disappointed if you don't* call." At this point, I guess it was clear that I was interested in John and he was interested in me—and my friend didn't mind at all. She was actually pretty excited for me.

So, the next day at work, I telephoned John. He sounded genuinely happy to hear from me. Since it was Friday, we were talking about our plans for the weekend. I told him I was going to see yet another band that night (we both worked in the music business) and asked what he was up to. He immediately said, "I'm going to see the same band." I could barely contain my excitement. I didn't know if he'd had plans to go all along or not, but my more optimistic side figured he was going just to see me.

When I got to the club that night, John was already there. He looked like he'd put a lot of time into getting ready. He looked great. We basically hung out all evening, getting to know each other. We were also drinking a lot, and the more we drank, the more sexual the conversation became. I asked if he'd ever had a threesome and he told me he had. He asked me what my biggest fantasy was, and I told him that I didn't have one in particular, but that I really wanted to get better at giving blow jobs. I swear, I think his eyes nearly popped out of his head. "I can help you out with that, if you want," he told me.

"Great," I said. "The thing is, my very first time doing it, the guy I was with kept correcting my technique—he told me I was doing it wrong. Ever since then, I've really wanted to prac-tice; I want to get really good at it." I think that was about the time we decided to leave the club and head to my place.

What started as something casual wound up becoming a six-month relationship. I now realize it was mostly based on sex, and even after we broke up, we slept together for another year. I was heartbroken at the time of the breakup, but I'm totally over it now. One of the things I learned along the way, *though, is that if I ever want to get a guy into bed, all I have to do is tell him that I'm looking to hone my blow job skills. It's just that easy.*

—Anastasia, thirty-eight, Brooklyn

## Drop Him a Line

In the final analysis, if you choose your words, your conquest and your timing wisely, it's our feeling that a pickup line—perhaps not in the most conventional sense, but a pickup line nonetheless—can be incredibly cool when it comes from a girl. Some of our favorites:

- "Did you order the lap dance?"
- "This place sucks . . . and so do *I*."
- "I'm on the rebound."
- "I'm a stripper."
- "I'm a flight attendant."
- "I like threesomes."
- "Me so horny."
- "I'm married."
- "Sex. Now."

## Lose These Lines

And then there are the lines you should obviously avoid at all costs. Let's run through some of those, just to be on the safe side:

- "What's your sign?"
- "I don't like raisins, but I'd sure love a date."
- "Is that a [name of phallic object] in your pocket, or are you just happy to see me?"

- "Let's rearrange the alphabet and put U and I together."
- "I want a boyfriend sooooooo badly!"
- "Why don't any men find me attractive?"
- "Are those space pants? 'Cause your ass is out of this world."
- "Are you from Tennessee? No? Well, you're the only 'ten' I see!"

# Step 3: Attitude

Ultimately, when it comes to getting a little action, an absolute sure-fire strategy lies entirely within your control, and that, dear ladies, is self-confidence. It's going to come through in how you view the world, the guys, and, most important, yourself. So how do you achieve that? There are so many ways.

1. Love Your Body. Here's the deal: guys like girls who are comfortable with the way they look. There are a million different kinds of guys and they are attracted to all kinds of women. So believe that you've got it going on and you're going to do just fine between the sheets. If a guy is flirting with you, and it progresses to casual sex—guess what? He likes the way you look, so work it like you own it, honey.

2. Be a Little Mysterious. As our friend Ruth, twenty-three, of Los Angeles, says: "No one ever plays with the puzzle once the pieces have all been put together. Take a hint, people. Complication is sexy. Stand naked in front of every peephole, and pretty soon people are going to get bored and ask you to put your clothes back on." Again, don't be like the game-playing "rules girls" who leave a guy completely confused (and a lot of guys confuse easily)—but

do leave at least a little bit up to his imagination. No reason to lay all your cards on the table before you lay him.

3. Make Eye Contact. If you want a man, you can pretty much let him know that with one long, hard look. Take in every inch of him with your eyes, hold his gaze, and then, just before you break contact, give him a small knowing smile. For bonus points, lick your lips and/or put something in your mouth (like a cherry or straw or olive). Chances are he'll be right over—as in, immediately.

And there you have it: whether you find yourself eyeing a guy who's easy or one who's a little tougher to pin down, it never hurts to have a few tricks up your sleeve. Think of them as your modern-day handkerchiefs, and drop them in front of him at will. In the best of all possible scenarios, he'll be bending over backwards to pick them up and take you home. If not, stick around and try again—we'd put money on the fact that there's a hornier and more worthy guy right around the corner.

**THE BOYS' CLUB SAYS . . .**

Girls hold all the cards, they decide when and where. A guy will very rarely say no to sex.

—*Frank, forty-seven, New York City*

*Could You, Would You*

*in a Car ... Or at a Bar ...*

*Or at Your Pad ...*

*Or at His Dad's ...?*

# Chapter Seven

# Where It's At

Sex in crazy places can be great. No, we don't mean in the butt. We mean the *location* of your lovin'. Now that you've carefully selected the right guy and avoided the wrong ones, figuring out where you do it may be almost as important as with whom you do it. This may even mean the difference between you getting exactly what you want or you not getting anything at all.

As we've addressed in previous chapters, there are certain essentials (the condoms, overnight kit, and so on) you're going to want to have with you when hooking up—but if you don't have them because you ignored our advice (you naughty thing), the place you end up could prove very important indeed. (That is, if you head to your place, you'll hopefully have everything you need at your fingertips.)

Furthermore, even if you do have the necessary munitions, it's important to head for a location in which you feel completely comfortable and are able to really let loose and have that night of unbridled passion for which you've been hoping. Finally, when you're talking casual sex, few things are worse than mid-act interruptions—so you'll certainly want to avoid destinations where you might have to deal with, say, roommates, parents, police officers, transients, and so on walking in on you.

On the whole, just about every scene will contain varying degrees of appeal. So, as always, it's up to you to assess the situation. Allow us to give you a heads-up on some of the finer points of the many popular casual sex settings.

RATING KEY:

★★★★★ = Ideal setting

★★★★ = Needs some minor repairs

★★★ = A move may be in your future

★★ = Relocation necessary

★ = You've got to be kidding . . . bail, and fast

Condemned = This place is beyond help

# Your Place

Generally, being in your own place has a lot of advantages when hooking up. For starters, you'll have everything you need to make yourself look and feel your best—before, during, and after the fact. And assuming you've planned ahead as instructed, you won't have to worry about whether or not he's got protection because you've got it all taken care of in your bedside drawer. In essence, you can be incredibly prepared.

Of course, as much as you may want a beautiful, homey place to lay your head, you may not be in that ideal situation just yet. Only you know if you've got the kind of pad in which you want to be entertaining a new friend. Is it going to make things more comfortable or less? The only other thing to consider is whether or not you want this guy to know where you live. Sometimes you may think everything's cool—or that he won't even remember where he was after the fact—but you can't always be sure of that. So, living in a secure building or, at least, a house with lots of locks is always a bonus.

★★★★★: You live alone. You can do it in the kitchen, on the couch, in the shower or bathtub—oh, and, of course, sleep comfortably in your bed afterwards.

★★★★: You have a roommate, meaning you'll pretty much have to opt for action in your bed—and you'll need to keep the moaning to a minimum (unless your roommate is used to it). On the upside, if things go wrong, at least someone will be close by to come to your rescue.

★★★: Again, you have roommates—yes, plural. Perhaps you even share a room or bathroom.

★★: Again, you have roommates, at least one of whom reminds you of that *Single White Female* chick, as well as a very possessive cat/dog/snake that loves to cozy up to any new man you bring home.

★: You have your own place—unfortunately it's a large cardboard box under the freeway.

Condemned: Sure, your place is great, but he's a stalker. Unfortunately, you didn't realize that until after you did him. The downside to bringing him back to your pad is

**THE BOYS' CLUB SAYS . . .**

Sex at the girl's place is the best idea. Chances are it's neater, and women feel better on their own turf.
—*Abe, thirty-four,
Los Angeles*

that you never know exactly how the evening's going to go or how long he's going to want to stay—in your place and in your life.

---

> **sexile,** v., to force your roommate to leave so you can have sex with someone you've brought home
>
> e.g., "I had a great time when I went home with Craig, but his roommates, who got sexiled, weren't quite as psyched as I was."
>
> **sexsylum,** n., The act of being taken in for the night after getting sexiled.
>
> e.g., "Hey, mind if I take sexsylum at your place tonight? My roommate just brought home a guy, and I've been sexiled."

## Setting the Stage

If you plan on entertaining at home, you'll want to have the following items at your disposal for optimum pleasure.

**Lamp or Lights with a Dimmer:** Nothing sets the mood—or makes your body look hotter—than softly dimmed lights. You can also opt for candles, although extreme sex (the kind that moves beds across hardwood floors) could translate this from fornication-friendly to fire hazard.

**Condoms:** We covered this in chapter 2. You haven't forgotten already, have you?

**Lube:** Water-based, please. If he's not getting you wet, at least this will.

**Water by the Bed:** A cup for each of you is a good idea. Not only will it keep you hydrated if you've been hitting the bottle—it can also serve as a brief breath freshener. And, if you're blowing him, taking a swig beforehand assists in lubing up your mouth.

A Fully Stocked Fridge: This should include beer and liquor for optional nightcaps, as well as coffee, tea, cream, sugar, orange juice, eggs, and bread—just on the off chance you can't get rid of him or feel like thanking him for a good night in the A.M.

Bonus Move: Scatter around a few napkins with guys' numbers or men's business cards (anything you've gleaned from previous conquests), so your man of the hour can see that you're the most wanted piece of ass in town. You might want to tear up one or two, so he can really see you're not relationship material.

## Going My Way?

If you decide to bring a guy back to your place, just make sure that you don't have anything immediately accessible that might allow him to take more from you than you'd intended to give him, whether it's a Tiffany bracelet on your vanity table, a new bottle of Vicodin in your medicine cabinet, or a journal full of your innermost thoughts, sitting right by the bed.

## Casual Sex Soundtracks

When the action's going down at your abode, music can also be an effective way to get yourself and Mr. Man in the mood and keep it entertaining. Some say it's cheesy and unnecessary to throw down the tracks, especially for something so fleeting. However, we find it can be appropriate on occasion, particularly if you practically define yourself by the songs and artists you adore. Depending on your disposition, decide who you want to be, and rock out with his cock out; it might go a little something like this:

### FINE TUNEAGE

Get his rocks off with songs that let him know who you really are . . .

- *Anglophiliac:* Morrissey, Cure, Charlatans U.K.
- *Bipolar Babe:* Tori Amos, Fiona Apple, Sinéad O'Connor
- *Soul Survivor:* James Brown, George Clinton, Isaac Hayes
- *Daring Dominatrix:* Nine Inch Nails, Hole, Prodigy
- *Fun-Loving Homoflexible (threesome, anyone?):* Ani DiFranco, Melissa Etheridge, Indigo Girls
- *Groovy Goddess:* Fleetwood Mac, Beatles, Cheap Trick
- *Ho, Ho, Ho:* Snoop Dogg, Queen Latifah, L.L. Cool J.
- *Nasty Narcoleptic:* Mazzy Star, Enigma, Queensrÿche
- *Party Princess:* Beastie Boys, Eminem, Cypress Hill
- *Postmodern Funkmistress:* Maxwell, The Fugees, Nikka Costa
- *Raging Rockoholic:* Jane's Addiction, Nirvana, Guns n' Roses
- *Sexy Sophisticate:* U2, Radiohead, Coldplay
- *Slutty Schoolgirl:* Britney Spears, Christina Aguilera, Jessica Simpson
- *Smooth Seductress:* Barry White, Al Green, Macy Gray
- *Trippy Hippie:* Grateful Dead, Pink Floyd, Blues Traveler

## SONICALLY SCARY

Want to get rid of him fast? Forget the hits and put on these sure-fire misses:

- *Maniacal Necromantic (graveyard, anyone?):* Rammstein, Marilyn Manson, Slipknot
- *Psycho-Stalker:* Alanis Morrissette, Avril Lavigne, Bjork
- *Crap-Whore:* Celine Dion, J. Lo (there's *not* always room for J. Lo), Mariah Carey

## CHEESUS CHRIST!

Depending on the dude, when you throw this down, it could go either way. So make sure you've accurately assessed the situation, and act according to what you want to happen—we, believe it or not, think this stuff rules!

- *Aurally Ambiguous:* Beth Hart, Suede, Queen
- *Fauxmantics:* Air Supply, Journey, Neil Diamond, Barry Manilow (bonus mention—you know we can't smile without him)
- *Delusional Diva (when you're not really sure if he's gay):* ABBA, George Michael (and Wham! of course), Culture Club

# His Place

The interesting thing about a single guy's place is that it can run the extreme gamut, from god-awful to pretty great. It's going to depend a lot on where your man is in his life. If he's youthful and energetic, you're probably talking frat house or dorm room—and there's nothing good about either of those. Avoid them at all costs. You don't want a college kid anyway. Go for a guy who's at least got some semblance of a career happening. In this case, you will be dealing with an apartment or, if luck has anything to do with it, a large and lovely home. Of course, apartment and house don't always equal independence. There's still the potential for the worst of all possible worlds: roommates.

These are just a few of the many reasons why you need to be sure to have your own car—or plenty of cab fare—if you decide to accept his invite to accompany him to his abode. The big bonus of heading to his place is that you've got the option of taking off at just about any given moment. (See chapter 9 for the details on extricating yourself from the situation after the deed is done.)

★★★★★: He lives alone in a palatial estate. You can go there, be comfortable, and take off as quickly as you like (plus, the souvenirs in the bathroom are most excellent . . . take a little something for your I-got-laid luau—and read more about that in chapter 10).

★★★★: Decent place, one roommate doing some chick in the other room—but at least there's a private bathroom, so you and your guy can still hit the showers together, before or after (or both). It smells like a guy's place, but at least there's toilet paper.

★★★: He has a studio apartment with a futon (or perhaps a twin bed, if the gods really aren't with you this evening), a television on a mail crate, and "dishes" that consist of paper plates and plastic cups in the kitchen. Sorry, did you want purified water to drink? All he has is a bottle of Coors Light in the fridge.

★★: He has roommates, a smelly dog, and bongs scattered around the house. If you don't get out now, not only will he be humping you but the dog will be humping your leg—and the guy will be so stoned, it will just make him laugh.

★: It's pretty much the same as the 2-star scenario, except for an added bathroom bonus: No, that's not a bath mat, it's a layer of pubes that have been collecting and gathering dust for the past five years. Oh, and you didn't need toilet paper, did you? Good.

Condemned: He's psychotic and has no intention of letting you leave—ever.

## *Go Clepto!*

Souvenirs, anyone? Sure, we said you should make sure the guy doesn't rip off anything from your abode, but that's mostly because we know how easy it is to do. If you wind up at his place, by all means take a little something to remember him by—not necessarily anything pricey, though. You can even ask him if he minds if you take it. That will make him think you're a clepto-psycho, so you're guaranteed to never have to see him again. As they say, the best things in life are free.

### SEXCAPADE:
## Oh, Brother (Or Was That Cousin?)

*In college, I spent the night at a fraternity on campus. It was a small school and, sadly, fraternities were the basis of our social life. It was around dawn that I woke up and snuck out. The sun was just coming up, the birds were chirping. It was too early for most people to be awake, so I thought I could make it back to my dorm without getting busted. I was wrong. There I was, hair a mess and wearing a guy's sweatshirt over my outfit, when who do I run into? My ex-boyfriend—the one who was heartbroken when I dumped him a few weeks earlier. The worst part was I had spent the previous night with his cousin! They happened to go to the same small liberal arts college. Don't ask me what he was doing up at that hour; probably a reverse walk of shame.*

—Sarah, thirty-five, San Francisco

## SEXCAPADE: The Stench of a Woman

*My biggest piece of advice if you wind up at a guy's place— or really, no matter where you go—always carry matches. I'll never forget the time I wound up at this guy's condo when, suddenly, I had a shooting pain in my stomach. I spent the next ten or fifteen minutes in the bathroom, emptying my bowels. Not only was I mortified that I'd been in there so long, but the smell I created was absolutely toxic. Normally, if I'm at my place, I have a matchbox somewhere near the toilet, which helps get rid of the smell almost instantly. Unfortunately, I couldn't find anything—not matches, not even some cologne or other nice-smelling spray. It kind of ruined the mood because all I could think about was how soon he'd be heading in there to discover the stench I'd left behind. Mortifying.*

—Cassandra, forty-one, Jersey City, New Jersey

## SEXCAPADE: Bachelor Party

*I went out drinking with some friends one night. After a couple of hours, one of my friend's boyfriends, Shane, arrived with his roommate Jeremy. I'd met Jeremy once before at a party* and we'd hit it off. I think we actually passed out on the same couch, but being passed out, nothing wound up happening.

Anyway, Jeremy and I began flirting and had a really great time talking to each other . . . but then he and Shane said they were supposed to be meeting up with some other friends, and they took off. I was bummed. I told my friend Karmen that I thought Jeremy was looking good that night, and she said we should just head back to Shane and Jeremy's—maybe they'd head home soon. Karmen had a key to their place, so that's what we did.

It was a decent house, but typical of a bunch of single guys. There were dishes piled up in the sink, and the place smelled a little—like single guys' pads do. Karmen and I made ourselves a couple of drinks, watched TV for a while, then headed to Shane's room to hang out. We were so tired, we wound up falling asleep on Shane's futon.

About an hour later, there were a couple of guys in the room trying to wake us up. It was Shane and Jeremy. Shane was telling Karmen to go to the living room with him, at which point it was just me and Jeremy. Before I knew what was going on, Jeremy was kissing me. Within minutes, he had my clothes off and was going down on me. A couple of minutes into that, he ejaculated. "Oh, man, I'm sorry," he said. "You're just turning me on so much." Generally, I expect that's the end of the performance for the night, but he just kept going. Five minutes later, Mr. Happy was back at attention, Jeremy reached for the condoms, and the sex was on—very on.

I think we must have gone a couple more times before falling asleep. An hour or two later, we were starting to wake up, and I felt bad that we'd left Shane and Karmen without a place to sleep. I shook Jeremy and asked him if we should get out of that room. "Yeah, probably," he said. So, we headed into his room where we crashed on his, uh, mattress on the floor, under a thin blanket. That's when Jeremy's enormous dog decided to come over and start nuzzling and drooling on me. As if the mood hadn't already been ruined by the makeshift bed, this was really putting a damper on things.

"Um, I gotta go to the bathroom," I said. At least he had his own. Of course, there was no toilet paper, so I did what I had to—I used the washcloth. Sorry, man . . . but ladies need to wipe! Then, I stumbled out into the living room to find my purse; I was in need of some makeup. When I got out there, I saw two other guys—I have no idea if they lived there or not, but they obviously didn't hear me coming and were startled when I caught them going through my bag. "Hey, kids, I'm the skank who slept with Jeremy last night," I said, figuring I may as well make light of the situation. "Can I have my purse, please?" They laughed like they were a little embarrassed, but I think they were actually stoned. (Why stop partying if it's only eight in the morning, right?)

I went back to Jeremy's room, told him I should probably go, and went to find Karmen. I told her I was going to grab a cab, and headed out of there.

The funny thing is, even with all the grossness of this bachelor-house setting, I still found Jeremy to be kind of endearing—and a good option for action. We wound up getting together a few times after that. It was purely a sex thing, and it was always at that house. I just made sure I could get out of there when I needed to. I even carried toilet paper (okay, tissues) with me, and I accepted the fact that he lived in a house full of guys who knew exactly why I was there. I'm sure I wasn't the first—or the last.

—Saffron, thirty-five, Hollywood

# Room at the Inn

There's something very appealing about having casual sex in a hotel—whether it's the guy's room or your own. If it's his room, just as with his place, you can pretty much come and then go as you please (pun intended). If it's your room, you can make up all kinds of excuses about being there for business and having early-morning meetings, and just kick him out. It's generally easier to kick a guy out of your hotel room than out of your house or apartment—and the added bonus is that the guy won't be able to track you down after the fact, so it's inherently stalker-preventive.

On another note, having sex at a hotel can be incredibly kinky in a good way. Since this environment is foreign to both of you, it often helps to lower inhibitions and turn you into the kind of sex kitten you've always wanted to be. You're not surrounded by your sleigh bed or your decor or the sheets that make you remember what a prude you usually are—so you can be someone totally different for the night, as can he. It's like casual sex Switzerland—neutral territory, where anything is possible.

The only issues that may arise have to do with the quality of the establishment (obviously the nicer the place, the better) and how you feel after the fact—as in, do you have a *Pretty Woman* complex? Getting a room for the night has certainly been stigmatized as a "call girl" thing, so that's a factor to consider and, hopefully, get over if you choose to go there.

★★★★★: He's got a room, he pays, you can leave as soon as you like. As sex columnist and author Anka Radakovich advises: "Always try to have sex in a five-star hotel. (And make him pay for it!)"

★★★★: You've got a room, hopefully he's not a psycho—but as with doing it at your place, you never know how long he's going to stick around. You may want him to leave a lot sooner than check-out time.

★★★: You're so hot for each other, you decide to get a room at a seedy motel—but at least they don't charge by the hour. "Never consent to having sex in a sleazy motel," says Radakovich.

★★: It's Motor Inn time . . . and you both wind up with crabs from the skanky sheets.

★: Neither of you has enough money for a room, so you decide to break into a hotel pool area, where you're promptly arrested for trespassing and public nudity.

Condemned: Not only does he take you to the Motor Inn, he ties you up as part of the kinky foreplay, then leaves with your clothes. That was supposed to be *your* plan!

## SEXCAPADE: Seasons Greetings

*Andy and I dated for a while when I lived in New York, but the most serious thing about the relationship was the sex (which was amazing). Six years after we went our separate ways, I got a message on my answering machine: "Hey there stranger, it's Andy. I'm in L.A. for a couple of days, and I'd love to see you. I'm staying at the Four Seasons. Why don't you come and meet me for a drink—seven o'clock in the lobby bar?" A hotel, a bar, and a hot man who'd be leaving in a day? I was there.*

*I knew I was in for some action when, a few sips into my second martini, Andy mentioned he had the Pam and Tommy Lee video upstairs in his room. "Have you seen it?" he asked.*

I hadn't, and I was just curious and tipsy enough to agree to a private viewing. I must admit it was some of their best work to date—and what editing!—but I didn't get to see the whole thing, since Andy and I got a bit distracted and created a few X-rated scenes of our own (off-camera, that is) before passing out.

I woke up at about 4 A.M. and began the mad search for my clothes. I threw on my tight black miniskirt, low-cut black sweater, and sexy slingbacks in the dark and quietly slipped out of the room. I wasn't feeling guilty, nor did I regret hooking up with him; I just wanted to make a swift exit, get to my car, and go. I thought I was home free as I pressed the lobby button and surveyed my freshly tossed hair in the elevator mirror.

No such luck. When the doors opened, I was blinded by what felt like a 400-watt lightbulb. As my eyes adjusted, I realized, there wasn't just one light but about thirty, accompanied by a camera crew getting ready to shoot the exact spot where I stood. I'd always dreamed of being in the movies, but this was a nightmare come true. Standing there stunned, I tried to figure out how I could exit gracefully. I took a deep breath, ducked my head, and stepped into the light. I snaked my way cautiously over piles of cables and equipment. So far so good, I thought, until—about twenty feet from the lobby exit—"Hey! Jamie? Is that you?" It was Bill, my old college boyfriend. I'd heard he had moved to L.A. to work as a movie grip.

I slowly turned and gave him an awkward hug, praying I didn't reek of sex. "What's up? Are you staying here?" he asked. I looked at him with my mascara-smudged eyes. "No," I stammered. "I was … just visiting a friend." It slowly registered on his face what kind of visiting I was doing. I could hear the *phone calls to mutual friends, "Dude, I so busted Jamie leaving a hotel at 4 A.M. post-coitus," and the banner at our reunion would read "Jamie Is Putting Out Now."*

*I tried to talk myself down. So I hooked up with a guy in a hotel; it's not like I was charging by the hour—and not only was it a nice place, it was a good time.*

—Jamie, twenty-eight, Beverly Hills

# Automobile?!

Ever since the car was invented, it (particularly those with roomy backseats) has been a popular place for all kinds of sexual adventures. But while going vertical in a Volvo—or getting down in a Durango, hitting it in a Honda (you get the picture)—can certainly be a convenient option if no actual buildings are available, and the thrill of doing it in a place where you may get caught can be an added turn-on, not all cars are exactly conducive to optimum comfort. Then again, there are the autos of the SUV, limousine, and van variety, among others, that are almost as roomy and comfy as an actual bed (perhaps even more mack-friendly if the other option is a futon). The scariest thing to deal with is the guy who actually appears to live in his car— you know, the VW Vanagon with the curtains on the windows? The toughest part of the average car is that it really only allows you to get into foreplay positions—if that. Actual person-on-person intercourse often proves incredibly difficult.

★★★★★: A large, cushy limousine or some other chauffeured affair, where everything is immediately accessible and neither of you have to get behind the wheel (and there's plenty of room for him to get behind you instead).

★★★★: It's your car. It's roomy and pretty exciting, since it's sort of sex in public.

★★★: He's brought you back to his vehicle of love, and it's clear you're not the first. Essentially, it's like the bachelor pad on wheels, with the pet hair and odor to match.

★★: Sportscar. Not only is he riding you—you're riding the hand brake or stick shift (or both). Suddenly, you know what it feels like for all those porn stars in the D-P scenes (double penetration, for those of you not in the know: Yes, we mean concurrent anal and vaginal intercourse).

★: On a parked motorcycle. Sure, it's pretty erotic, but aside from freezing your ass off, chances are good that someone's going to see you and/or arrest you.

Condemned: You're steaming up the windows, when the cop comes over and hauls you both off to jail—but not before checking to see if you've been brought in for soliciting in the past.

## SEXCAPADE: Auto-Erotic

*One weekend I was in Ocean City, Maryland, with a group of my girlfriends. I was on the outs with my then-boyfriend and decided that, since I had never had a one-night stand, I was going to go for it that night. We went to a club with a real beach feel—sand on the dance floor and all that. We were there for about twenty minutes when I met this hot softball player from Philadelphia. We were flirting with each other all night, and when he was ready to take off, I offered to drive him back to his hotel. He informed me on the way that he was sharing a room with two other guys, so we decided to pull into a parking lot off the main strip for some action.*

*He was a great kisser and had a hot, hard body. The only problem was that neither of us had a condom, but I was so worked up I couldn't stand it and I decided to finish myself off before I exploded. I just started masturbating in front of him, which was apparently a huge turn-on for him. He sat there watching and groaning as I finished. Then I got dressed and dropped him off—never even got his name.*

*You'd think the story would end there, but it doesn't. After picking my friends back up, the one whose car I'd taken to drop off the hot guy was acting very strange. In fact, she would barely talk to me. When I finally confronted her, I learned I wasn't the only one who got off that night. Apparently Mr. Not-So-Soft balls finished himself off as well—probably while I was getting dressed—and my girlfriend had sat in his leftovers on the front seat. Luckily, we laugh about it now.*

—Amy, thirty-one, Fort Morgan, Colorado

## Sexcapade: Lady Picture Show

*I was set up on a blind date by a friend but, as with any blind date, you never know what to expect. When I opened the front door, I must say I was not disappointed: my date, Carl, was tall, dark, and hot. The plan he came up with was miniature golf and a drive-in movie, which I thought was adorable.*

*I knew we were on the road to sex on the third hole at the golf course. He stood behind me to line up my putter and gently leaned down on my back and whispered, "You're driving me crazy." It was a ballsy move, but it worked: I was wet right then and there.*

*By the time we got to the drive-in, I knew exactly what I wanted: him. We steamed up the windows with some heavy petting and then went for it. After we were both satisfied, he turned to me and said, "Truth or dare?" Considering what had just transpired, I went for dare. I figured he'd made a strong enough move already, so what could possibly take things further?*

*"You have to let me drive you home, with both of us completely naked," said Carl. Not being one to turn down a dare, I told him to go for it, and we hit the road. It was ten long miles to my house, and I can't say I've laughed any harder in my life. I'm just happy we didn't get pulled over by the cops.*

—Paula twenty-eight, Burlington, Vermont

# Sex in Public

Whether it's bumping and grinding in the great outdoors or getting raunchy in the nearest restroom, who hasn't fantasized about—if not acted upon—certain exhibitionist urges? It could quite possibly be the ultimate fantasy: the sun has just set over the waves (or mountains . . . or dumpsters), you've just shared a bottle of wine (or Bud . . . or Pabst Blue Ribbon)—and then, nature takes its course in the midst of nature itself. There's also the possibility that you're at a public place— a bar or other festive locale—and your only option is to slip away to the lavatory-of-love when no one's looking. If there's a lock on the door, you're good to go.

Sadly, these fantasies rarely live up to reality—not in all cases, but often enough. Why? Well, first, it's virtually impossible to expect that you'll get all the way to the end without interruption. And second, unless you have everything you need to make the setting cozy and comfortable—whether that's enough blankets and an absence of sand or grass in your ass, or finding enough toilet seat covers to make yourself a sanitary mattress—going public, in general, is probably a lot better in theory than in practice. As Pamela, thirty-one, of Riverton, New Jersey, notes in the simplest terms possible: "The beach is too messy and bathrooms are too dirty. I don't recommend them."

★★★★★: You're at a party which just happens to be in a mansion. You escape to the master bathroom where there's a Jacuzzi tub for two and thick, luxurious towels as big as sheets. After you take a nice, hot soak together, you get out, and he bends you over the marble vanity. You watch yourselves climax repeatedly from every angle in the floor-to-ceiling mirrors.

★★★★: He owns his own island, there are no other inhabitants, and there is a beautiful bed located under a canopy just far enough from the shore where you can make mad, passionate lust from dusk till dawn. Of course, this would never happen, which is why it gets four stars instead of five.

★★★: You go to a nightclub and the women's bathroom line is the good old mile-long cliché. Since there's no one in line for the men's (as always), you decide to hit one of the stalls in there. Just then, a super-hot stud walks in. It's on. Within minutes, he's behind you, your face to the toilet and his back to the stall door. The only problem is that the door keeps swinging open as guy after guy walks in on you—and let's not forget about the stench of urine and the yellow dribble all over the toilet, just beneath your jiggling bosom.

★★: Sex on the beach revisited. But this time, you can't decide which part is most romantic: the wind in your hair (which is chilling you to the bone), the sand entering every available crevice in your body, the rocks in your back, or the beachcomber who's picking up bottles and checking to see if there's anything left in them worth drinking.

★: Same as the 2-star, but the beachcomber decides what you're doing is more fun and jerks off as he watches you.

Condemned: Same as the 1-star, except that the cops come and arrest all three of you—at which point you get to know the beachcomber even better than you could ever have imagined.

### SEXCAPADE: Standing Ovation

*The best one-night stand I ever had was with this guy I'd just met. We were driving along the coast in Los Angeles, and as he rambled on about something, I found myself wanting to see him naked right then and there. He and I drove to the beach and we strolled a while. He stopped me suddenly, and we started making out in the middle of the beach. The Lakers were winning, so people were shouting with joy from their beach bungalows until they saw us and proceeded to root us on.*
—Meegan, twenty-four, New York City

### SEXCAPADE: Oh, Henry!

*It was the season finale of the TV show* Sex and the City *and my gay friend Todd invited me to a "farewell to the fine and freshly fucked ladies" party he was having. He said I could bring a friend, but we had to promise we would adhere to his dress code: bedroom attire all around—the racier the better. I knew my friend Donna didn't get out much, so I asked her to join.*

*We arrived at the restaurant that Todd had rented for the night, wearing our outfits pour la boudoir. Donna went for a tight black nightie and a pair of smokin' hot "knock me down and do me pumps" and I chose to wear my hot pink bra and panties with matching see-through robe. I also wore some high, strappy sandals that gave me a long set of porn-star gams. I must say, we looked fine.*

*The party was in full swing when we arrived and the place was decorated to the nines. (The gays sure know how to throw a soirée). All the tables had gigantic martini glass centerpieces with candles floating in pink liquid. The tablecloths were leopard print, and there were TV monitors playing episodes of the show in every part of the room. All signs were pointing to a good night to score. There was only one problem: no straight men were invited to the party. I mean not one.*

*Todd said he was so sorry, and he felt really bad that he hadn't even thought about our needs. As he was apologizing, an incredibly hot waiter appeared, and I said to Todd: "Typical, hot gay guy—what a waste!" But Todd scoped out the situation through the manager and found out that not only was waiter-boy straight, but there was also a gorgeous—and very hetero—bartender on duty. All we could do was hope they were not only waiting but ready, willing, and able to service us.*

*Donna and I decided, between ourselves and our homo homies, who should go for whom, and thank goodness, I chose Henry the bartender. Donna started her work on the waiter, and after two cosmos got him into the bathroom. She returned sooner than any of us would have expected, announcing that* she was going to bow out of our little pick-up-dicks game. She said the poor guy had started out just fine, but then he began licking her face and she had to bail.

Everyone at the table laughed, never thinking that the Sex and the City episode where Charlotte had to deal with an offensive kisser like that would be a reality, and Todd joked that now he definitely wasn't going to try to "turn him." Then, all eyes were on me, and Donna dared me to go close Henry. I was nervous as I approached the bar, but when I got there, I took a deep breath and started up a conversation.

I'm usually pretty subtle when it comes to picking up a guy, but it was getting late, and there was no time for subtleties. After a few minutes of flirting, I just plain went for it and gave him my pitch: "So, my friend and the waiter over there just made out in the ladies' room. Perhaps it's time for you to take your break, and we can do the same." I was stoked when he called the manager over and said he needed to take a few minutes off. I only hoped it was going to be more that just a few...

I let Henry go to the back and figured I would wait a bit before I joined him. As I was walking down the hall, I saw his silhouette by the back door. I grabbed his arm and led him into the ladies' room. Once I made sure the door was locked, I turned, leaned against the door, and gave him my come-and-get-me look. He was on me in two seconds flat. We made out for a few minutes and he was quite the opposite from his

*partner in crime. Henry could kiss, and pretty soon I thought I was going to explode.*

*Then he whispered in my ear, "This is what my tongue will do when I go down on you." He then proceeded to demonstrate on my mouth. Oh my God! That was the biggest turn-on for me ever. I had my first orgasm with my leg propped up on the sink while he hit me south of the border. Number two was leaning over the sink with him doing me from behind. I am not a multiple gal, so I was shocked when that happened—and then, somehow, between being in a public place and Henry's skills, I was able to hit a third.*

*After we were both satisfied, we washed up and made our exit. I returned to the table and handled the post-sex press conference like a pro. As I was inundated with questions, I just smiled and nodded yes to the fact that I got some and no to revealing any details beyond that. Todd giggled, then said he was glad the party had worked out and that I would have made the* Sex and the City *girls proud. In true Samantha style, I left the party that night without even a nod over to the bar, feeling proud indeed.*

—Fran, twenty-nine, Los Angeles

# Just Don't Go There

Now that you know the pros and cons of your location options, let's get down to the ones you should probably avoid at all costs. People are always bragging about the most exotic places they've had sex. Yeah, great. Sounds a lot more fun in the story than when you're actually on location. Meanwhile, in addition to be overrated, certain places are rarely appropriate for a one-night stand. Aside from the likelihood of interruptions, nothing particularly good can really come of these—at least, not usually. For instance:

## A Friend's Place

Sometimes this turns out okay, but not often. Basically, you need to have really understanding friends. And, no matter how great they are, chances are you're going to offend them, even if your guy-for-the-night doesn't leave his splooge on their new Pottery Barn couch. It's just poor form on your part. Do your best to find a better option.

## A Relative's Place (Yours or His)

No matter how liberal the household, who wants Mommy or Daddy, or sister or brother, or anyone else to hear what you're up to or, worse still, walk in on you? Your chances of avoiding interruption are, uh, relatively slim. So take it elsewhere, kids.

## An Airplane

The Mile High Club is such a cliché—not to mention incredibly overrated. You're not seriously going to try to hook up with a guy in that cramped little bathroom you can barely fit *one* person into, are you? Talk about uncomfortable. And really not all that hot. On the other hand, mutual masturbation under those tiny little blankets with a guy you've just met can be pretty great—so we'll give you that exception.

## An Elevator

There's nothing all that exciting about this—you're bound to pick up extra passengers, so there's never enough time to do it the way you want to. If you stop the thing, the alarm either goes off, or the thrill is gone because the thing's not moving anymore. How is that fun?

## *For Exhibitionists Only*

We've touched on the ideal and abhorrent possibilities involved in doing the deed in automobiles, public restrooms, and outdoorsy areas. For the truly adventurous couple that doesn't just get excited by casual sex but wants to take it one step further, there are a number of places where you might want to get busy. Allow us to offer some suggestions, with a few tips on keeping it hot, not bothersome.

**Art Gallery:** If anyone catches you, just pretend you're doing a live, nudist performance act.

**Dressing Room:** Make sure you're a bona fide exhibitionist, because the security cameras may not take your best side into consideration when the whole thing is captured on film.

**Hammock:** Maintain your balance and swing baby, swing.

**Library:** Shhh . . . sex is in session. Be sure to stay out of the children's section.

**Movie Theater:** Just remember that silence is golden. If you're a screamer, you should probably take in a horror flick and, of course, sit in the back row.

All in all, selecting the spot isn't nearly as simple as you might have thought, is it? When lust is the force steering you toward an encounter, you tend to forget about things like comfort—not to mention interruptions and, eventually, stalkers . . . all those silly little things that can turn a wonderful time into a wonderfully awful one. While certain locations can be part of the sexual thrill and a total turn-on, we recommend you always run down your mental checklist and decide whether or not the good will outweigh the bad or vice versa. Do you really want to ruin things by getting stuck in a dangerous or embarrassing situation? Of course you should do it where you want—just don't get caught with your pants down.

*Casual Sex Means*
*Never Having to Say*
*"I Love You"—And a*
*Whole Lot More*

# Chapter Eight

# Techniques, Taboos, Turnoffs, and Trouble

L adies, start your engines, because now we're getting to the nuts and bolts of the deed itself. We all know that casual sex is about getting off—and there are a lot of things you can do to not only score but make sure it's a full-on grand slam for you *and* him. Regardless of how many sparks have been flying up until now, if you've loaded up your sexual bag o' tricks with certain skills, you will not only be able to woo him but will, in turn, make him want to wow you.

## Techniques

There are certainly no hard-and-fast requirements; and it's really about what you want to do to him, and what you want him to do to you. As Dr. Ava says, "There are no rules about sexual techniques. Some women will not want to kiss their lovers for fear of getting too emotionally involved. Others won't give them oral sex because they only want to receive." Whether it's one night only or not, you should never feel obligated to do anything you don't want to do. That said, the fact that you'll probably never see the guy again may give you a completely new lease on lust.

In fact, a lot of women have told us that when they're having casual sex, they feel like they can be the kind of lover they've always wanted to be—that they never felt comfortable doing certain things with guys who knew them better. "A few times, I have felt more at ease and comfortable doing more adventurous things with a stranger," says Jenny, thirty-two, of Santa Cruz, California. As Cake cofounders Emily Kramer and Melinda Gallagher note: "Casual sex can be an opportunity to try out new techniques, positions, or fantasies. A one-night stand can also allow you the freedom to try out a new sexual persona—whether it be the diva, the vamp, the professional. You can speak her words and let your imagination flow."

Women who participated in our Happy Hook-Up survey also told us that they view casual sex as an opportunity to practice certain techniques they were never really sure they were doing well (as we saw with wannabe blow job queen Theresa in chapter 4 and Anastasia in chapter 6). So, first, figure out if the guy that you're going home with might be open to a little adventure—or if you will be. Then consider the various opportunities available to you.

Just be aware: You've got the opportunity to try a lot of things, and so does the guy you're with. Some of these may be welcome, whereas some may be off-limits in your mind, and you may need to make sure they stay that way in practice. There's also the chance that things could get pushed a little too far in the uncomfortable direction, and we mustn't overlook that either (more on that in a bit). For starters, let's run through some of the techniques you might want to explore and/or have in your erotic arsenal.

## Playing with Protection

Now that you find yourself in the throes of passion, it warrants revisiting the finer points of prophylactics as initially discussed in chapter 2—for now it's time to actually get it on (the condom and the coitus). While a lot of guys will whip out and roll on the rubber as fast as humanly possible (all the faster to do you with, my dear), there are going to be those times when you may need or want to provide a little erotically charged assistance. In fact—particularly if you're going to have protected foreplay (as every good doctor and sex expert will highly recommend)—you can make the love-glove part of those preliminaries. It may even spice things up if you do.

If the package is in your hot little hands, try ripping open the wrapper like a wild woman on a mission (just don't be so wild that you rip the condom in the process). You might then go with the traditional, tried-and-true roll it on with the hands option—or, for an even kinkier possibility, take it in your mouth and roll it down his shaft with your lips and tongue. This will likely require a bit of practice so you may want to try it on your own with, say, Mr. Vibey. (Don't get all red in the face; we know he's in a drawer in your bedroom.) You just need to make sure your teeth don't turn this into a more-harm-than-good situation; not only can your choppers tear the condom but they can be quite a painful blow for the guy. If you prefer to use a non-lubed condom for this tricky technique, don't forget to add some water-based lube before penetration.

For an extra special turn-on (if you're particularly dexterous), you can try to slide it on with your feet and/or toes. Again, we recommend a lot of pre-show practice for this method; you haven't come this far only to fail and look foolish, now have you? So, that's the creative stuff. Now let's go through the absolutes:

- Do have one or two condoms at the ready, in case he doesn't. (But only use one at a time; double bagging can cause the condom to break or slip off.)

- Don't bust out an entire case. (You want to be safe, not appear to be a pro.)

- Do insist on complete coverage before the penis is placed anywhere near your vagina, mouth, or anus.

- Don't let him talk you out of using one.

- Do pinch the tip of the condom and smooth the air out as you roll it on.

- Don't rub the lube all over his member before putting on the rubber, as this could cause the condom to slip off.

### Giving Direction

Whether it's his kissing style, the way he touches your body, his cunnilinguistics, or the sex act itself, you must be absolutely honest and sometimes aggressive when it comes to your satisfaction. There's nothing wrong with telling him what's working for you and what just plain isn't. His tongue twirling in the ear might have worked for his last conquest, but if it's feeling more like a slobbering, jamming mess to you, it's perfectly acceptable to pull away a bit and be ready to give him some gentle direction—verbal or physical. You can gently whisper in his ear "what really gets me hot is . . . x, y, or G." Not only will this ensure you get what you came for (literally), but will most likely be a real turn-on for him. Guys love a little dirty talk. And we all know the golden rule: "Do unto others as you would have them do unto you." So perhaps if you nibble his ear the way you want yours nibbled, he'll get the picture and adjust his technique. How else can you be guaranteed a good time?

- Do ooh and aah only when he's really pleasing you.
- Don't fake satisfaction when he's doing it all wrong (or he'll just keep going).
- Do guide his hands directly where you want them.
- Don't let him do anything that makes you uncomfortable.
- Do reciprocate when he's really getting it right.
- Don't focus so much on him that you wind up with lockjaw and little else.

## SEXCAPADE: Hot or Bothered?

*I was in my hot tub with this guy I had met that night at a party. We were making out and I was teaching him Pick your Poison—a game where you choose between two things, such as beer or wine, bottom or top, pain or pleasure. Mark wasn't great at the game and was having a hard time coming up with questions for me—but I realized he had finally graduated and got it when he whispered in my ear, "Pick your poison: Sushi or sex?" Stunned as I was, I smiled and replied, "Both please." He lifted me up out of the water and went down on me right then and there. The "sushi" was great, but the sex was mind-blowing.*

—Sasha, thirty-seven, Honolulu

**size queen**, *n.*, a woman who prefers a man's penis to be enormous—the bigger, the better

e.g., "Caitlin is a size queen, so when the guy she hooked up with last night turned out to be three inches when fully erect, she was out of there."

**penetration princess**, *n.*, a woman who enjoys intercourse over all other forms of sexual activity

e.g., "I don't really care if a guy goes down on me or not— I'm a penetration princess and would prefer that he just stick it in already."

## Going Down

Of course no man out there would decline a blow job, but he's also in no position to demand that you service him in that way—particularly if this is a casual encounter. So the question is, are you willing and wanting to go down on him?

It's all a matter of personal preference. A lot of the ladies who responded to our Happy Hook-Up survey admitted that giving head is something they do every time they hook up with a guy. "I give an impressive blow job—and I enjoy it," notes Veronica, thirty-five, of Los Angeles. "It also puts you in a position of power. These are all good things when you don't really know the guy. It makes him think you're a goddess."

Other women said they would never go down on a guy in a casual situation, claiming it's too intimate an act to perform with someone they don't know that well. Some also told us they just hate the thought of a cock in their mouth. "I don't even like giving a guy I've been with for a long time a blow job, so why would I feel like going down on someone I'm never going to see again?" says Melanie, twenty-eight, of Brooklyn. Bottom line: it's your call. If you *do* decide to go there, here are some not-so-sucky suggestions.

- Do have a glass of water nearby—you may need it before, during, and definitely after.

- Don't hold your breath or let your mouth get too dry. Make sure you have enough saliva flowing.

- Do try sucking on a breath mint (or swigging a little mouthwash) a few minutes before working on his member. The minty sensation has been known to give guys a jolt of pleasure.

- Don't go too fast. Tease him with your mouth and tongue. He may want you to get right down to it, but make him wait and he'll want it even more.

- Do apply long, licking strokes from the base up, rather than short, quick licks.

- Don't feel obliged to deep-throat. The tip and head of his member are the most sensitive areas, and men generally say that focusing on that portion is perfectly fine with them.

- Do relax your neck and throat. You'll be less likely to gag if he's in fact big enough to hit that spot (for your sake, we hope he is).

- Don't forget to use your hands.

- Do learn what the taint (the spot between his boys and the butt) is and apply moderate pressure with your fingers. You're sure to get a nod and moan of approval.

- Don't allow him to climax in your mouth, let alone swallow. Use a non-lubed condom when giving head. Flip to appendix 2 for more about the STDs you can get from having oral sex. If you really feel you need the protein, go get a Clif Bar.

**taint,** *n.,* also known as perineum, *n.,* the area between a guy's balls and rectum or between a woman's vagina and rectum—often said to be a sensitive area that many people (men in particular) enjoy having stimulated. Some say it is thusly called because "t'aint your genitals and t'aint your butthole," while others note that it stands for "The Anus Is Next to This."

e.g., "Josh's erection nearly doubled in size when I touched his taint."

### SEXCAPADE:
## Just Put Your Lips Together and Go

*My friend Pam and I were watching a movie one night, and her mother sat down with us and started watching. There must've been some reference to a blow job, because Pam's mom suddenly came out with, "I've never really known what that means—what is a blow job?" An awkward moment of silence followed, but she didn't let up. "I mean, do you literally blow on it and kinda kiss it?" I was so embarrassed I had to leave the room. I didn't want to be there to listen to Pam give her mom the blow-by-blow.*

—Carlotta, thirty-two, Wichita, Kansas

**pope-sex,** *n.*, also known as Clinton's legacy, sexual activity that stops short of actual intercourse

e.g., "I'm saving myself for the man I marry, so I only have pope-sex."

# Getting in Position

When the foreplay's finished (we would have instructed you on cunnilingus, but we figure you're probably pretty clear on how that's done—and hopefully he is, too), it's time to cleanse the palate with a swig of water and get on to the main course. Whether he's bending you over the kitchen counter to take you from behind, you're riding him like a stallion, or even taking it the plain old missionary way, casual sex is a great opportunity to strike a variety of poses and discover the ones that really get you off. Here are some quick tips to make the most of the biggies (simply follow these dos and don'ts for the most part, regardless of the specific position you find yourself in):

## Missionary

It's the good old meat and potatoes with him on top and you on your back—but that doesn't mean it has to be bland and boring. Since this is usually the springboard to start everything off and often the final position for the big finish, put a little effort into making it work *for* you, not against you:

- Do thrust your hips up and around.
- Don't just lie there and let him do all the work.
- Do tighten your PC muscles (remember how we taught you to do this in chapter 3?); not only will he feel you closing around him for his own pleasure, but you'll feel him more, too.

- Don't spread your legs so wide that neither of you can feel anything.

- Do wrap your legs around him or even place your lower legs on his shoulders for deeper penetration (placing your feet flat on his ass will cause his pubic bone to rub against your clitoris, while throwing your feet over his shoulders will really get him in deep).

- Don't let him go so deep that you hurt yourself.

## Doggy Style

Another classic position—him behind and you on all fours—allows him to view you from behind (and men just seem to love that visual). Although, as with the missionary, it may seem he has all the control, that's not necessarily the case. You can also make it about your satisfaction in a variety of ways, while keeping the less desirable aspects of it at bay:

- Do pleasure yourself manually while he goes at you from behind.

- Don't be embarrassed to masturbate in front of him—he doesn't even have to know.

- Do make sure you're on a soft surface. Your knees will thank you.

- Don't injure yourself on hardwood floors, dirt, sand, or rocks.

- Do have him pull out from time to time. Reentry feels great.

- Don't allow him to "slip" and go anal (if you *do* want him to go there you need a new condom).

## Woman on Top

Why do so many chicks dig this one? The answers obvious: he's on his back and you're in control (either face to face or you with your back to him, sitting on his lap). Since you can be as aggressive as you like from this location, you'll really be able to manipulate his genitals and yours—which is why so many women have the easiest time achieving climax this way. "To enjoy casual sex: relax, have fun, be the ball, and *stay on top*," agrees Ruth, twenty-three, of Los Angeles. If you're not sure you've got it in you, so to speak, just take note:

- Do be aware of pacing and vary it. Start slow, speed it up, then go back to slow.

- Don't just wildly jump and hump him.

- Do allow him to rub your breasts—or massage them yourself.

- Don't become self-conscious about how you look—he's *very* happy with it.

- Do allow yourself to climax, repeatedly if possible.

- Don't let him slide out of you, which may cause you to land on his cock wrong (a major injury may ensue).

---

**SURVEY SAYS . . .**

Woman-on-top is America's favorite sexual position, according to the 2003 Durex Global Sex Survey, with rear entry (doggy style) coming in second.

---

SEXPRESSIONS

**spinner,** *n.,* a small girl—about five-foot-two or shorter; if she were to be on top during intercourse and you simply flicked her, she'd spin around like a nut on a bolt

e.g., "John wanted to get Debbie into bed because he's into little chicks who ride him—and she's definitely a spinner."

circus sex, *n.*, sex without using protection—as in working without a safety net; can also refer to bizarre sexual behavior of any kind

e.g., "That guy wanted to have circus sex—no condoms and lots of spanking."

# Taboos

Some people find that sex with someone they're not in love with is taboo—but if you've got this far, clearly you're cool with that. Still, that doesn't mean you'll be an *absolutely anything goes* kind of girl, and you don't have to be. You can determine where your line is, and make sure that the man of the hour doesn't cross it. Be aware that because you're up for a casual romp in the first place, he may make certain assumptions about what else you'll be willing to do—so it's going to be up to you to set him straight as promptly, convincingly, and firmly as possible. Don't bend your rules just because he's presumptuous enough to think his wish is your command. As we've said, no one should expect you to do anything you don't want to do.

Of course, we've also noted this may be the time when you *do* want to push your boundaries a little bit—try things you'd never try with a more familiar guy. Some women take that to an extreme and actually go for the taboos, full force. "I enjoy trying things out on people I may never see again. It's a little freeing," says Marsha, thirty-five, of Saratoga, New York. "In fact, the best anal sex I ever had was with a one-night stand when I was out of town. I picked him up in a bar and we went to a hotel room. He was an ass guy and he had his mouth and hands all over me for hours. It was very nasty and very fun. I don't know if I could ask for that from someone I knew better, but I hope so." On the other hand, our friend Ruth, twenty-three, of Los Angeles, says quite simply: "Casual plus anal equals no." Obviously, once again, it's up to the individual.

The important thing is to lay down the law before you lay *him* so you're both clear about what you will and won't feel comfortable doing. "Ground rules can be very exciting if

**THE BOYS' CLUB SAYS . . .**

Stay out of my rectum, and I will stay out of yours.
—*Larry, twenty-seven, Berkeley, California*

they are presented in the right way," says Dr. Ava. "You can tell him what sexual activities you will and won't indulge in and even tell him that you want to have your orgasm first." Just so you're prepared for the gamut of kinky requests or attempts that may enter into the equation, we'll run through some of the more prevalent ones.

- Anal sex: Getting to boogie in your butt is something most men are going to try for all kinds of reasons (we keep asking what they are, and that's when they seem to shut down). If you're game, make sure he's got a condom and plenty of lube and he goes verrrrry slowwwwwly or it could be a serious pain. Also, remember you need to change condoms when going from anal to vaginal, and vice versa, to lower the risk of infection.

- Cock rings: They will make him last twice as long—which is great if he's worth that much time to you.

- Cuffs and stuff: If you must go there, just make sure *you* have the key. And don't let it get too violent—bondage and all that goes with it can be a scary reflection on who you're dealing with. "One time I was hooking up with a guy I met at a club in the parking lot and he started asking me to whip him," says Pamela, thirty-one, of Riverton, New Jersey. "I left immediately. Too weird of a request from a stranger."

**THE BOYS' CLUB SAYS . . .**

In a casual sex encounter, I'm expecting the fundamentals. If there are indicators that it could get a little wild—more and more positions, talking dirty, adding toys—that can be great, but it's not expected.

—George, forty-six, Bethesda, Maryland

- Facials (not the kind you get at the spa): Chances are he wants to come all over your face because the girl in his favorite porno seems to enjoy it so much. It may be a thrill for him, but would he be so thrilled if you squeezed ranch dressing up his nose or—worse still—in his eye? Probably not. But you decide where you want the money shot, honey.

- Golden showers: We're hoping that he's the one who wants you to pee on him, and not the other way around.

- Sex on the rag: Some guys don't mind it, and if you don't either, then more power to you. Just make sure the tampon's not in—and you should probably only attempt it on the lighter days. One guy we know opted to go for it, even after being told the girl he was with was menstruating. Afterwards, he went to the bathroom and let out an ear-splitting scream: "Oh my god! It looks like I was *wound-fucking* you!" he said. Amazingly, the sheets stayed clean.

- **Sex toys:** If he's *almost* getting you to the point of nirvana, but not quite, perhaps you'll be needing a little help from some vibrating friends. Just prepare yourself for a mixed reaction. He'll either be utterly delighted or completely horrified and disheartened by the fact that he alone couldn't satisfy you.

- **Spanking:** A nice slap on the ass can be fun, but as with the anal penetration, too much could impair your ability to, oh, let's say . . . sit down for three days. And you'll be reminded of this naughty night of passion every time you catch a glimpse of his handprints on your backside for the next week as well.

- **Videotaping the action:** You're finally starring in your own movie, but its big premiere might end up all over foragoodtimecall.com. We think it's best to leave the hardcore movies to the pros.

---

**SURVEY SAYS...**

According to the 2003 Durex Global Sex Survey, 49 percent of Americans have used vibrators and/or sex toys and 33 percent have used handcuffs or bondage equipment.

---

## SEXCAPADE: In Through the Out Door

*I'd known this guy for a couple of years through a friend we had in common, and I always kind of got the impression that he liked me and I liked him, but we never really had the opportunity to be alone. Then, one night, we ran into each other at a bar, and after drinking all night, I invited him back to my place. We wound up having really hot sex. I was pretty drunk, but I remember him starting to put his dick in my butt. At first, I told him to stop, but he went all the way in and pretty soon we were having full-on anal sex.*

*We slept together a couple more times after that, but it never wound up leading to a relationship. In retrospect, I really wish I hadn't had anal sex with that guy. I've only ever had it once before, in a very serious relationship, and my feeling is that it really has no place in most sexual relationships—especially casual ones. I actually think it's kind of weird that so many guys I've been with want to go there.*

—Simone, twenty-four, Detroit

---

SEXPRESSIONS

---

**rimming** or **rim-job,** *n.,* stimulation of the anus with one's tongue, sometimes referred to as shit-eating (for obvious reasons)

e.g., "When Joe asked me for a rim-job, I told him to eat shit (because I sure wouldn't)."

# Turnoffs

Most of the time, the things that turn you—or him—off are things that you can't even plan for or avoid. These are often on par with some of the date-stoppers mentioned in chapter 5, and sadly they transpire when you're already in the middle of the action. Maybe you'll be able to escape just in the nick of time; maybe you won't. All we really care about at this point is the fact that these situations can make for some damn funny stories—and aren't we really all here for a little amusement? Then let's get started . . .

## Turnoff 1: Hurling

*Tom and I dated off and on throughout our high school and college years, and we've remained close since then. We had many mutual friends, and one night we all made plans to go out to dinner at the Culinary Institute of America for a seven-course meal. The food was tremendous, and so were the wines we paired with our meal.*

*As the courses and the evening continued, so did the old sparks between me and Tom. I know it had something to do with all the alcohol, which does it to the best of us, but I also really valued the intimacy Tom and I had shared together through the years, and I grew more and more nostalgic as the hours passed.*

*After our excellent meal, Tom offered to drive me home. He stopped at the end of my street and asked if I wanted to get out and take a walk since it was such a beautiful night. The moon was full and all the stars were out, and soon we found ourselves under this huge pine tree, leaning against it and taking off our clothes. As we rubbed against each other, I found myself getting down on my knees, so I could take him in my mouth.*

*I'd only just started to lick and tease him when I felt my meal rising up. Then, the top of his penis caught the back of my throat, and a seven-course meal was now spread all over his jewels. I was never more embarrassed in my life, but Tom was so nice about it. He managed to clean himself up as best he could, got me on my feet, and walked me to my door, making sure I was okay before he kissed me on the cheek and said good night. We're still friends to this day, and we've never spoke of it since.*

—Steph, thirty-two, New York City

## Turnoff 2: You Want *What?*

*I was once with this guy who couldn't get hard, let alone climax, without his nipples being pinched and twisted really hard. I spent the whole time in bed working on his nipples, and I couldn't relax and enjoy myself. He never even asked me what got me off. After a few sessions, I called it quits. He kept calling me and wanting to hook up, but I felt his bedroom behavior was so selfish; I left him twisting in the wind.*

—Laura, thirty-four, Riverton, New Jersey

## Turnoff 3: Jackhammering

*My most disappointing one-night stand was with a guy who was one of those poundpoundpound lovers, like a jackhammer, with no foreplay or nuance. I faked an orgasm to get him off of me. He said, "You come like a hurricane." Ewwwwww. Where did he get that line from, an eighties hair band? It was so disappointing—he had been so suave with his clothes on. When we were done I said, "Okay, well, I'll see you later," and kicked him out.*

—Diana, thirty-one, Chicago

## Turnoff 4: Mr. Softy

*One night, while out with some girlfriends, I met a really attractive guy. Since I was a little tipsy—and horny—I invited him to come home with me. His name was Dylan and he seemed very excited by my direct approach, so we we left. After about 10 minutes of making out at my place, we got naked. Unfortunately, about 5 more minutes into it, I realized that Dylan had had way too much to drink . . . he was really floundering, and every time he tried to penetrate me, he lost his erection. After a half hour or so, we silently agreed to go to sleep.*

*The next morning, Dylan told me he had to get to the set of a movie he was supposed to be filming (yes, he was an unknown actor). I told him I'd drive him. As we walked out to the car, he grabbed my hand, held it tight, and gave me this sheepish grin. I don't know why he looked so pleased with himself—it's not like he'd been the king of all lovers or, really, like he'd even been into me (literally) as far as I* know. He must have just been putting on some kind of act, so I wouldn't feel used or something. The funny thing is that I'd tried to use him, not that I got anything for it.

So, I dropped Dylan off, and he asked for my number. I don't know why I gave it to him, but I did. Less than a week later—2 A.M. on a Friday night—I got a phone call. Sorry—booty call. It was Dylan. I didn't pick up. He left a message: "Hey Angela, it's Dylan. I think you know why I'm calling." He left his number. Even though I was kind of psyched and flattered he called, I didn't call him back. Why would I when he hadn't delivered the first time?

—Angela, thirty-one, Hollywood

**THE BOYS' CLUB SAYS . . .**

I guess having a girl vomit is kind of a turnoff. That happened once during oral sex. It wasn't a size thing; she was really drunk and I guess I touched off her gag reflex. Kinda hard to get the sparks flying after that. But the biggest turnoff for me? Tears.

—Monty, forty-one, Spokane, Washington

## Turnoff 5: The Early Bird

I once had casual sex with this young boy from Brooklyn. He got off before me, so we did it again. He got off before me again, and I said, "I told you to tell me if you're going to come!" His reply: "Sorry, next time I'll hold up a flash card." Not only was he a dick for coming too soon—twice—he was an asshole about it to boot.

—Sheila, thirty-seven, Syracuse, New York

### THE BOYS' CLUB SAYS . . .

One turnoff is apologizing. I don't give a fig if your "room's a mess" or your "roommate's a bitch." I am not here to judge. Relax for Christ's sake. Pulling a Paris is another turnoff. That's when a woman does something so totally rude, acting like one of the Hilton sisters, such as answering her cell phone while we're doing it. Then it becomes obvious that this isn't casual sex; this is unfriendly acting out. I guess women do it to feel like they are getting over on a guy. No one likes feeling gotten over, boy or girl. Another thing that is just unnecessary: porno talking in the sack. I love a little dirty talk, but it's very easy to overdo and comes off as disingenuous. Also, after a while I lose respect for gutter-mouth users.

—*Chuck, thirty-four, Cleveland*

## Turnoff 6: Snooze-o-Rama

*When I was in college in London, I met a wealthy older gentleman. We went out on a couple dates, and he lavished wine and food and treats on me. We finally got nasty, and it was monotonous and boring. Yawn. I was hoping he would kama sutra me or something, but it was just a total letdown.*

—*Linda, thirty-two, Los Angeles*

# Trouble

Turning you off with his unusual or otherwise unappealing sexual preferences is one thing—but getting creepy or scary or introducing you to his psychotic tendencies is something quite different. If he can't get it up or perform to your liking, you can just chalk it up to bad experience and move on—but the more serious side of casual sex is one we can't ignore altogether: when good times go bad.

We've done our best to provide you with some insights and advice on how to make sure you select your lay and location with caution, to use your good judgment and trust your instincts. But, doing all that still doesn't guarantee you won't be out with Bipolar Boy. If, at any point, the red flags go up and warning bells start ringing, you're going to need to come up with some solutions and perhaps an effective exit plan. If he's being disrespectful, if he gets trashed and turns belligerent—whatever it is—you'll need to think fast, be smart, and do whatever it takes to get out of there or send him packing.

We've already addressed some of the ways you can ensure your safety and protection—by carrying your cell phone, having your car with you, and letting friends or family members know where you're going to be. Here are some other potential scenarios that could—and have—cropped up for certain girls we spoke with and insights on how they dealt with the dangers of casual dating:

## Nightmare Dot Com

*I once went out with a guy I met on an Internet dating sight. I was relieved when he showed up and was almost as cute as his picture. I drank several glasses of wine while we had a really nice dinner and conversation and, by the end of the date, I had decided I'd like to have sex with him. So, I invited him back to my place.*

As soon as we got there, he came up behind me and indicated he was ready for action. We went into my bedroom and started having sex, and suddenly he turned into a completely different guy. He was grabbing my hands and holding them pretty tight, trying to manipulate me into positions he wanted me to go into. At first, I went with it but said something raunchy that I thought might get him to let up a little. Instead, he freaked out and said, "Why are you talking like a whore? Why don't you just keep your mouth shut?" I did my best to comply, as I really started to sense that this was not the kind of guy I thought he was.

Afterwards, we were out on the couch, and he said, "At what point did you decide I was only good for one thing?" I really wanted to shoot back that it had been something I thought we'd mutually decided, but I could see he was determined to put me in my place, and I didn't want to set him off. So, I played coy and dumb and told him that I'm just a bad, confused person and I was really sorry if I'd done something to hurt him. "Hurt me?!" he said. "No bitch will ever hurt me, baby." Yikes. How was I going to get this guy out of my apartment?

As the conversation wore on, he started uttering all kinds of racial slurs. I was getting more uncomfortable by the moment. Honestly, I don't even know how I made it through that morning. But, fortunately, after a couple of hours of odd conversation where I just tried to agree with the guy and build up his ego, he said he had to take off, but that he'd had a great time and that maybe we could see each other again sometime. I told him to call or email me and we'd figure it out.

About a week later, he emailed me to see how I was doing. I emailed him back and said that I felt really bad about how things had gone and realized I just wasn't relationship material and hoped he understood. Fortunately, that was the last I heard from him. Of course, the more fortunate part is that I didn't wind up in a ditch somewhere, after taking the guy home with me in the first place.

—Saffron, thirty-five, Hollywood

## The Aggro Asshole

*My worst sexual experience was a date I went on a few years ago. The guy was gorgeous and sexy, and I had this feeling he was going to be really good in bed. When we got to the parking garage and into his car and started making out, he was all over me. No nuance, no building up to the act. He was so aggressive. I kept telling him to slow down, but he wouldn't. It was like he was in fucking heat. He kept trying to shove his hand down my pants while pinning my arms over my head. When he tore my shirt open, I'll admit I was scared to death. I just wanted to get out. I kept struggling, but I couldn't get my arms free. My only defense left was my legs, so I kneed him in the balls, which put him into the fetal position. I ran from the car and kept thinking, thank God we were in a semi-public place and I didn't go home with that twisted little fuck.*

—Natalie, thirty, Baltimore

## Kinky Meets Creepy

*Nearly ten years ago, I was out seeing a band in Hollywood with some friends. Towards the end of the night, this tall drink of rock 'n' roll godliness—I mean, seriously fine—saunters over, and within five minutes, we're headed back to my place. (An absolute record. I've had my share of one-night stands, but it's not exactly a habit.) He followed me on his motorcycle, and I laughed the whole way home.*

*Once home, we had pleasant, if rather unremarkable, sex; and then he wrapped his hands around my neck and began squeezing— as in asphyxiation. I sputtered and demanded to know what the fuck he was doing, and he was like, "Babe, trust me, you're gonna love it." Needless to say, visions of my dead body being discovered the following day by my roommate filled my head, and I told him that under no circumstance whatsoever was he to touch my neck, thankyou-verymuch.*

*I can't tell you why it didn't cross my mind to run screaming or at least give him the boot from my bed/apartment, but I passed out next to a potential serial killer that night. In the morning, under better light, I also realized he was the guitarist in a bad late-eighties hair metal band. He lazed around on my couch for about an hour while my room-mate and I became increasingly nervous about his ever leaving.*

*In retrospect, I knew this guy wouldn't kill me while I slept, but for the first time, I realized that when you engage in a one-night stand, you really never know for sure whom you're dealing with. It behooves us ladies to practice a little caution. I'm usually a pretty cautious person with other people, but this one sealed the deal. He obviously wasn't the Hollywood Strangler—but he could have been— and now that I live alone, I don't think I would ever bring a complete stranger home. Even if he were as hot as this guy.*

—Lana, thirty-four, New Orleans

## Unhappy Accidents

*The year was 1985. I was twenty-three and just discovering my sexual identity. One night at the club Limelight (a club in an old church, and the address was 666 Sixth Avenue—creepy!), I was danc- ing to my favorite Modern English song, "I Melt With You," when this really cute punk boy started dancing with me. After the song ended, we headed to the bar to get a drink and the flirting began. Appropriately enough, he had that Nicolas Cage in* Valley Girl *kind of look—a real bad boy, which was just my type. He told me his name was Patrick, and he lived on the Upper East Side. I thought that was strange—he looked so downtown—but what the hell, he was into me and I was into him; addresses didn't really matter.*

*We made out in the club for a while, and then it started getting too hot and heavy for public viewing, so we grabbed a cab and head- ed off to his place. Once in the cab, we were all over each other. He* had his hand up my skirt and I was unzipping his jeans when the cab pulled up to his building. He threw the driver a twenty, and we headed up to his place, where we got it on not once but twice. Both times, I was very careful and conscious of making sure he wore protection. The next morning (or afternoon, actually), he walked me out, gave me his number, kissed me on the cheek, and hailed me a cab.

I left not knowing or caring if I would see him again. I got what I went for—in truth, as it turns out, a lot more. Nine days later, I woke up in such excruciating pain I was doubled over. It was like I was being stabbed in the gut, and after an hour in the fetal position on the bathroom floor, I stumbled to a cab and headed to the emergency room. I was petrified. The doctor started the exam and asked if I had had sexual relations lately. I told him I had, that it was about a week ago, and that we used protection. "Yeah, I see that you did," he said as he pulled the rubber out of me! It had been in me for days and had caused a major infection.

I was so pissed and angry at Patrick for not telling me. Where did he think it went? The doctor gave me antibiotics and told me I needed to go to my gynecologist for a full Pap, STD, and pregnancy test. What I really wanted was to give Patrick a fuckin' Pap smear myself. When I got home I called my doctor and then dug the asshole's number out of the bottom of my bag. He answered the phone and said he was really glad I had finally called him.

"Not so sure you're going to remain happy after I say what I need to say to you." Silence. "Did you notice something missing after our second go-round?" I asked. Silence, again. "Well," he stammered, "I wasn't sure what happened to it, and I didn't know what to do or say." I was so furious. I yelled, "I just got home from the emergency room, where they had to remove what you left behind! I only hope you get a nasty infection, like the one I have." Then I slammed the phone down and headed out to the doctor.

*Fortunately, I recovered and all the tests came back negative, but I learned a huge lesson that night. Now, I literally do a condom check and count after sex. Some men find my behavior strange, but screw them. Oh wait. I probably just did.*

—Amanda, thirty-nine, Nashville

# Your Exit Plan

If you find yourself in a sketchy situation, how do you get rid of the guy or stop him from mistreating you, mid-act? You may have to just work through it (as some of the women in the preceding stories did) say the experts. You don't want to risk upsetting a violent guy who might turn even uglier at any given moment. Always use your head, assess the situation, and do what seems most appropriate at the time. Sex therapists and psychologists also offer these slightly more sobering insights on getting out of an unsavory situation.

1. **Shed some light on the subject.** Lean over and turn on a lamp or flip on the light switch. The sudden shift in setting and mood may be enough to make him lose his focus—and his erection.

2. **Just lie there.** Don't talk, don't move, and be as inanimate as possible—even to the point where you feign passing out or begin snoring. The lack of action on your part may help to put an end to his interest in continuing.

3. **Fake an illness.** Scream or yell as though you're in terrible pain, then indicate that he's hurting you or that you just got a shooting pain in your abdominal region. Run to the bathroom, perhaps even pretend to throw up, then tell him you'd better leave or ask him.

4. **Laugh it up.** If you can muster a few giggles or more, your lack of seriousness could serve to turn the guy off. Apologize as you continue to laugh, then tell him maybe you should just go—or ask him to leave.

5. **Leave the room.** Stop the action and tell him you need to go to the bathroom. Stay in there for at least ten minutes, by which time he will likely have lost his interest and/or his erection. Then you'll be able to leave or ask him to.

6. **Tell it like it is.** Say straight up that you're not attracted to him, that you're finding his behavior off-putting, or that you just need to leave (or that he does). Be as direct as possible.

In the final analysis, there's a fine line between pleasure and pain—and in a casual encounter, you're the person who has to decide what that fine line is. Do not, under any circumstances, do anything you're not comfortable doing. The safest and most practical way to enjoy yourself and have a good time, rather than allowing a good time to turn ugly, is to take charge, be responsible for your actions, be in constant communication, and never be afraid to say what's on your mind. Tell your man of the hour what you like and—more important—what you don't like. If his behavior alters in the appropriate direction, you've succeeded, and so has he. In the best of all possible worlds, he will adapt to your needs.

On the downside, if you feel threatened or disrespected, get out of there and learn from the experience. As with the less serious but still unsettling date-stopper situations discussed in chapter 5, there's nothing wrong with bailing on a bad encounter. It's not worth losing your dignity—or worse still, sacrificing your safety.

*You Came (Hopefully),*
*You Saw, Now How Do*
*You Make the Break?*

# Chapter Nine

# The Girl's Guide to
# Humping and Ditching

Well, just look at you with that after-sex glow, smiling like the cat who ate the canary. We feel like proud parents! Clearly you got what you came for, and hopefully you came and came and came, avoiding any of the turnoffs or trouble mentioned in the previous chapter. But now, what are you going to do?

When it's all said and done, to successfully complete your casual sex mission, you've got to get out as gracefully as possible. If this was a true one-night stand, chances are you won't want to see the guy or hear from him again—at least, you certainly don't want to put yourself in that vulnerable position. After all, things are never as easy as you may like to think you've been, now are they?

No matter whom you hooked up with or where the deed went down, what happens next is going to play a tremendous role in how you feel about yourself, him, casual sex, and the days and weeks that follow. So you must play the minutes and hours after climax carefully. Believe it or not, some guys actually want to make you their sexual slave . . . one of many booty calls in their little black book. Don't give them the satisfaction, and don't let them call the shots. It's all up to you, and your ultimate goal should be to make this end here and now before things get complicated. A few hours with the guy is fine . . . go beyond that, and you're looking at a giant can of worms (they're phallic for a reason).

You can even plan ahead and make it smooth sailing, way before the game even begins. "I suggest that before you have sex with the guy, you tell him he has to leave after you're done with him," says Ruth, twenty-three, of Los Angeles. Of course, hindsight is always 20/20, and this is simply one way to approach it. If you'd prefer to leave the post-encounter events more open-ended, you're going to have a lot of decisions to make. But you're used to that at this point, aren't you? Don't worry. We've got you covered.

# To Spoon or Not to Spoon?

Immediately after the sex, if you're in a bed or near one—or even if you're not—the temptation is almost always going to be to snuggle up with someone. Whether or not you like the guy—even if the sex wasn't spectacular—it's often a simple matter of conditioned physical behavior. Have sex, then spoon (or at least pass out next to each other). Unfortunately, this can often be a bad idea.

For starters, spooning is relationship-type behavior, and deeper feelings may soon follow. Plenty of men and women actually steer clear of spooning with anyone after a casual encounter, and it has nothing to do with how they feel about the person they've just done. They're not repelled by the person's smell; they don't think the other person was bad in bed. It's not a reflection on you or the kind of person you are, so don't even let yourself think that way.

Leaping to the other side of the bed, room, city, state, or country just happens to be a defense mechanism that men, in particular, tend to master more effectively than women. It helps to keep those emotional walls up and that closeness from creeping in. There are those rare occasions when he will be a soft, sensitive, snuggly kind of guy, but don't expect him to be—and don't be the one to initiate that sort of behavior. *Never* give him the touchy-feely satisfaction when you've already satisfied him enough. Our friend Parker tells us that it's something you have to put out of your mind completely:

## SEXCAPADE: Casual Sex Laws

*The first few times I had casual sex, the guys were really nice and seemed to want me to crash there. Sometimes I did, sometimes I didn't … it was always my decision. Sometimes we snuggled, sometimes we didn't—I was generally a little too drunk to recall whose decision that was.*

*Then, I had this one guy who I saw a few times. He was so passionate and into it while we were in the midst of the sex, but then he would be on the opposite side of the bed when it was over—seriously, like as soon as I came, it was as if I was covered in some sort of repellent.*

*In retrospect, I now realize that he was just a casual sex veteran. Not only would he not spoon—we rarely made out or made eye contact. After encounter number three, even though I tried to set up a fourth session, I never heard from him again. Live and learn. Now I know the rules, and if you're aware of them and you follow them, you're pretty much clear on how things work, and you never let it fuck with your head again.*

—Parker, thirty-seven, Los Angeles

# Post-Coital Conversation and Crashing

As with the spooning, there's also the chance that you're both going to be so energized by what's just gone down that suddenly you can't shut up. You start talking and laughing, and suddenly—oh no!—you're bonding. Bad idea.

As with spooning, you're venturing into relationship-like, wanting-to-see-him-again territory here, and that is not your goal, nor should it ever be when having casual sex. "The most successful casual sex relationships are those where the couple doesn't talk much after," says Dr. Ava. "Don't get into a conversation about your problems or his problems. Don't ask too many questions about his family, work, hobbies, friends, political views, etc. The less you know about each other, the better the sex will be." Indeed.

As Diana, thirty-one, of Chicago, says, "I can have casual sex without becoming emotionally attached only if the guy is a jerk afterwards (or if he's not very good in bed). If he's a gentleman, treats me well after the fact, asks me to spend the night, and he's also good at pleasing me, then it's near impossible to stay emotionally unattached." Diana's advice: "If you want to stay clearheaded emotionally, do not let him talk to you or romance you afterwards, and, above all, do not spend the night!"

# Get Up and Go

So, what do you do if you can't spoon or talk or sleep over? Aren't things going to feel a little awkward—and how do you deal with that? "There is no way of guaranteeing that there will be no awkwardness after having casual sex," admits Dr. Ava. "But you can get up, wash, and leave as soon as possible so that you can avoid too much conversation." This really is the best way to prevent virtually any discomfort that might come up. "Leave before sleeping or before the other person wakes up if your intent is to not see that person again," agrees Pamela, thirty-one, of Riverton, New Jersey.

Unfortunately, that only works if you're at his place or a place where it's easy to vacate—which, as we said in

**THE BOYS' CLUB SAYS . . .**

When it's all said and done, and it's time to part ways, I generally just say, "See you at school—don't forget your books!"

—*Randy, thirty-seven, Boston*

chapter 7, is one of the bonuses of steering clear of your own pad. Sure, you could still get up and leave if you're at your own place—but you probably don't want to leave some guy you don't know very well in your home, unattended . . . do you?

# Get Him to Go

If he's at *your* place and—God forbid—seems like he's intent on sticking around for a day or more, things could start to get a wee bit problematic. If you really want to get rid of this guy, the key is to be honest, direct, and to the point. If you don't want him in your bed, you need to tell him to go. It doesn't have to be harsh, it doesn't have to be cruel—it can just be what it is.

If you're able, most women and experts recommend sarcasm with just enough seriousness. "Say 'Thanks for a great lay—now shouldn't you be on your way?'" says Becky, twenty-two, of Lansing,

Michigan. Veronica, thirty-five, of Los Angeles, adds that a little laughter can go a long way: "To make things less awkward after the fact, I highly recommend humor," she says. "Being open and funny, from the very beginning, is the way to make any situation easier. If you can't be like that, then you probably shouldn't be doing this."

We also like the story about the girl who takes a Polaroid of every guy she's done to lighten up the send-off. "I whip out my camera when he's still lying there, naked," says Raquelle, twenty-three, of Atlanta. "I make him think I want a picture because I'm so hot for him—then, after I look at it, I say 'thanks for the memories . . . let's make that all that's left.' If he doesn't get it, I tell him I have trouble sleeping with a stranger in my bed, so would he mind going. That usually works like a charm." Later, you can write his vital stats and any details about your night of passion on the front or back of the photo (including how he performed) and keep it for your casual sex celebrations (see chapter 10).

# So Long, Stranger

The hope is that the guy, just like you, will simply want to get up and be on his way. Even if it feels like a slam at the time, his departure is a *good* thing. Remember, this was not the man of your dreams; this was not the guy you will be spending the rest of your days, weeks, and life with. Stop questioning why he left, what you did to drive him away, and accept that it's a blessing—he's doing you a mitzvah, as members of the Tribe say. If he bolts, be grateful. Just ask Marni:

### SEXCAPADE: There He Goes Again . . .

*I was at a party that my cousin threw and, as usual, had too much to drink. I was feeling sassy. I was the sexy older woman;*

*these kids were just out of college and I was "almost thirty." I was wearing my favorite Chinese platform sandals, and there is nothing like a badass pair of shoes to make a girl feel invincible. I love going to parties alone and, after a few drinks, have no problem walking up to groups of people that look interesting and making myself a part of the conversation.*

*There was this amazingly beautiful guy (whose name I don't know to this day), and after chatting for a while (about what, I have no idea), I said, "So, are you coming home with me, or what?" Remember the book The Rules? As if.*

*So, come home with me he did. I could lie about the sex and tell you that it was amazing, but honestly, I just don't remember. I do remember thinking, every thirty seconds, that this is the hottest guy I have ever slept with. It usually doesn't matter to me—the face, the body, any of it—but for some reason, in this case, the way he looked was the thing that made me tingle straight down to my toes.*

*He spent the night, and when I woke up in the morning, I noticed that he wasn't in bed. So I wandered around my apartment, looking for him ("Here, hottie-hottie, here boy . . . !"), and found him standing in the kitchen. I asked him if he was leaving, and he said no, he had just gone to the bathroom. Okay. So I go to the bathroom, and when I come out, he is gone.*

*I felt bad for like thirty seconds—but in reality? My feeling is he saved us both from the weird morning-after discomfort. We didn't have to deal with any of the "what do we do now?" crap. I, at no point, had any intention of seeing him again, so it was basically a win-win situation, and a relief that we never discussed anything afterwards, nor crossed paths.*

—Marni, thirty-four, Chicago

# Is He Still There ... And Are You?

So, you did the unthinkable and slept with the guy—as in, did him and then you both stuck around. Okay, all is not lost. We've got a backup plan for you. In fact, sometimes it's kind of fun to stay put and see how weird and annoying things can become. If you want to get him to leave you alone for good, you can try your luck with some of the offensive behavior our Boys' Club buddy Richard mentions on the next page. Here are some other little pearls we've picked up along the way. Just make sure that, if you're not an actual psycho who makes men want to slit their wrists, you're going to have to really sell these lines. So put on your acting pants, look him directly in the eye, and deliver these like you mean them:

- "I'm having brunch with my parents. Care to join?"

- "I'm so excited that I have a new *lover*. And what an amazing *lover* you are ..."

- "*Making love* with you last night was incredible. Did you feel the earth move like I did?"

- "If you're going to send me flowers now, make sure they're not carnations."

- "Want to go to church [or temple] to worship with me?"

# Breakfast in Public

If you're not lucky enough to sneak out, have him sneak out, or drive him off with your scathing wit before any conversations transpire, then you're dealing with a whole lot of post-encounter possibilities, the most obvious of which is the morning-after meal (generally break- fast ... but, of course, it depends on what time of day you hooked up with the guy). So, how are you going to handle this one, little lady?

This is basically your opportunity to play the I-got-action role to the hilt. Unless you did it at your place—and have all your accessories, a change of clothes, a shower and hairdryer and fresh make-up and all the rest—going out in public looking the way you do is simply going to scream "walk of shame." But you can put the *ham* in shame—and no, we're not talking about breakfast meat . . . you got enough meat last night as it is.

We're talking ham it up, have a laugh, look at this as a fun-filled morning, to be your Flirtiest, post-Fornication Femme Fatale—all with capital Fs. Why? Because you got *fucked*, and more power to you. Let this man know that

**THE BOYS' CLUB SAYS . . .**

The morning-after drive to get coffee (ten minutes max) has been suicide-inducing with many of the women with whom I have had casual sex. Do I want to hear about your plans to start a band? That you think David Lynch movies are, like, weird? That some other chick at the strip joint put a hex on you because she's a Sagittarius? Hmmm, no.
—*Richard, thirty-seven, New Orleans*

there is nothing for you to be ashamed of, and then parade him around the nearest diner like a prize pony. Got it?

## Call Me ... Or Don't

The next consideration in the whole aftermath is dealing with the infamous phone number exchange. What if he asks for your number? Be very wary of giving it to him. He may insist on calling you when you have no interest in seeing the poor sap again. He may even start harassing you and hitting you up for more sex—and that can be a royal pain. "How do you get men to stop with the booty calls? I will only have casual sex on my terms—not his. Why don't they get this?" moans Ruth, twenty-three, of Los Angeles. Here's what Ginger learned about giving out her number, a little too late:

## SEXCAPADE:
## The Earth Moved (Too Bad I Didn't)

*It was a Sunday night. The next day was Martin Luther King Day, a holiday, so my best female friend and best male friend, who happen to be fuck buddies on occasion, and I headed out to find some bad music, smoke machines, trailer trash, and alcohol—not necessarily in that order.*

*As we were drinking and dancing to Tone Loc, Dee-Lite, and Aerosmith, I spotted the only good-looking guy in the place. He was gorgeous. I didn't think to wonder why he would be caught dead in there, mostly because I didn't want him to wonder the same of me. I tried all night to get his attention. I am sure I caught him looking at me once or twice, but he never approached me. So we closed the place and headed out to the parking lot. While walking to the car, I saw my target—and he saw me. I believe he called me over like a dog, but I went eagerly, regardless.*

*Within minutes, he had my phone numberand his tongue in my mouth. Game on. One hour later: he (who shall remain nameless because I don't remember it) and I were sport fucking at my place. I'm not sure where my other two friends were, but I figured they were doing the same, somewhere in my apartment. We finally fell asleep.*

*At 4:30 A.M., my world began rocking again—harder and rougher than the three previous times. I realized it was an earthquake. Mr. X and I leapt to our feet and took cover under a doorway. It seemed like forever as we waited for the shaking to end. I felt close enough to him to take comfort in his arms as I tried to get my bearings.*

*Amid all the confusion, I barely heard the knock at the door. My friends were outside. My door was blocked by a fallen bookshelf and they couldn't get back in. Mr. X couldn't get out of there fast enough—I think he said something about getting home to check on his roommate, but who cares?*

*Now I don't have a problem with one-night stands. But I do prefer that they remain just that. After the earthquake, many people were left without electricity and water. I was fortunate to have both. Mr. X was not so lucky. Unfortunately, he had my number, so he called daily asking if he and his roommate could use my shower. Jesus Christ, doesn't this guy have family he can call?*

*I don't remember when he stopped calling (probably once services were restored), and I will probably never remember his name, but I will always remember that night for as long as I live.*

—Ginger, thirty-two, Malibu, California

# The Phone Number Exchange

So here's the deal with the whole "can I get your number?" issue post–casual coitus: Your best-case scenario is to take his number *but do not use it.* Why? You may need to contact him if he's given you an STD, but beyond that, getting his number and then calling him puts the power in his hands. The last thing you want to do is give him the impression that you're desperate for him when you're really not (are you?). If you take his number and don't call, he'll be the one sitting by the phone.

Unfortunately, if you give him your phone number, there's a chance that you may develop those awful expectations, and *you'll* start waiting by the phone, wondering why he's not calling you to go see a movie or grab dinner or just screw. "If it's a pickup, let it go,"

**THE BOYS' CLUB SAYS . . .**

I think asking for someone's number is just good manners. You might never use it, and you should be prepared to be given a fake out number, but always ask.
—*Pete, thirty-three, Alexandria, Virginia*

advises Marsha, thirty-five, of Saratoga, New York. "Don't give him your number. It was fun, it was one night, let it be a pleasant memory." Do not start fantasizing about the fact that he desperately wants to make you his new American-style girlfriend. (How many times do we have to warn you about this expectations stuff?)

You should also realize that sometimes a guy just asks you for your number because he doesn't want to seem like a dick who just used you for sex (poor thing doesn't realize you just used him for his dick). To make sure that you don't wind up pining, we recommend that you practice the following, so you have no option but to put him out of your head and realize you won't hear from him:

- Only give him one number (home is fine; he doesn't need your work, cell, pager, and fax numbers)—and make sure you have caller ID. If he calls, let it be an ego boost, but *never* answer it; let him leave a message and keep the recording as part of your one-night-stand collection (see chapter 10).

- Get out of giving him your number with one of the following lines:

    > "Why? What are we going to do—*date*?"

    > "I just moved and I don't remember it."

    > "Um, yeah, I'm not really good with numbers..."

    > "Why don't you just give me yours? I promise to call you, like, every day."

    > "My shrink says I'm an enabler, and I'm trying to work through that; so, I'd rather not enable you to stalk me."

    > "What's a phone number?"

    > "No."

- Practice the "one digit off number" (your number, with one incorrect digit). It will be fun to see if he can solve the mystery! If he does, maybe he's worth seeing again...

- If you're constantly getting asked for your number by losers you don't want to deal with, consider memorizing your local "rejection hotline" number (find it at rejectionhotline.com).

When the guy calls this number, he will get a recorded message telling him he's just been rejected. Brilliant! (We're also big fans of some of their merchandise—like the thong that says, "Just because you got my clothes off doesn't mean you're getting my real number.")

## The Phone Number Exchange Translator

| | |
|---|---|
| If he says: | "Can I get your number?" |
| *He means:* | "Can I get another blow job?" |
| If he says: | "Can I call you sometime?" |
| *He means:* | "Can I telephone you at midnight next Friday for a booty call?" |
| If he says: | "Can I see you again?" |
| *He means:* | "Can we have sex again?" |

# The Pickup Artist

If you've done the unthinkable and given him your real number, look at it this way: you're lucky the gods invented voicemail. Of course, if he calls and you accidentally answer it (in spite of the fact that you don't want to see him again), you've still got time to correct the gaff. How?

- Act like you have no idea who he is.
- Speak a foreign language.
- Pretend you're your own answering machine and beep at the end.

- Tell him you're seeing a few other guys this weekend, but you might be able to squeeze him in next month.

- Pretend-cry and tell him you can't believe he waited so long to call you (even if it's only been a day).

- Say you're on the other line with a sick relative and ask if you can call him back ... then don't.

- Ring your own doorbell over and over and tell him someone's at your door and you've got to go.

- Frantically whisper that your husband's home and insist that he never call there again.

- Fuck it ... just hang up and screen more carefully in the future.

Now, don't get us wrong—we certainly don't mean to imply that your whole goal here should be to ditch the guy or treat him like dirt. After all, he gave you something you wanted (hopefully), and for that you should politely thank him. All we're saying is that you don't need to belabor the thing or drag it out any longer than necessary. If you've been clear with your conquest about why you're there, he should understand and move on, just as we're hoping you will. The whole point is to appreciate the moment—celebrate it (as we'll outline in the next, and final, chapter)—and then strut on out of there without looking back. Go your separate ways, call it a day, and keep on keepin' on.

*You Got Laid!*
*How to Live It Up and*
*Not Lament It*

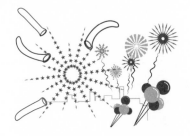

# Chapter Ten

# Celebrating Your
# One-Night Stands

We began this book by telling you that being single is not something to whine about, but rather something worth celebrating, and we're going to go out on the same note. After all, at this point, we've pretty much exhausted the topic of casual sex as one of a single girl's greatest opportunities, and the hope is that you've discovered a way to tap into your passion and power, and you've reaped the rewards with absolutely no regrets. You got what you wanted, you did it the safe, smart, and satisfying way, and for that, you need to do nothing but pat yourself on the back, party, do a little victory dance, and go on with your bad self.

One of the most encouraging things we discovered in our research was that women are finally feeling pretty damn good about themselves after having casual sex. In fact, they're just about on par with the men. Among the over one hundred people who respond-ed to our Happy Hook-Up survey, 29 percent of the women and 32 percent of the men said they generally feel sexy or attractive, and 11 percent of both the women and men generally feel empowered, after doing the ephemeral deed. Not too shabby.

Unfortunately, 16 percent of the women and 11 percent of the men feel guilty, and 3 percent of the women and 11 percent of the men report generally feeling depressed after having casual sex. Furthermore, 87 percent of the women and 95 percent of the men told us they'd regretted having casual sex at one time or another. No wonder we had to write this book. In the name of no regrets, people, even if it wasn't all you'd hoped for, even if things got a little weird or awkward—hell, even if something horrifyingly scary happened—guess what? You are a more enlightened individual for it.

These feelings of fault, sadness, or remorse are relatively worthless, aren't they? How far do they really get you? We say, look at what's gone down as an opportunity, instead—an opportunity to be a wiser, stronger, bolder, and, yes, even happier person. Some bookstores are placing us in the self-help section after all, so let's just go for it right here, right now: love yourself, ladies! You done him, and therefore you done good! Lots of the girls we interviewed agree that it's the best head-space possible. "I've actually been very proud of myself after casual sex," notes Veronica, thirty-five, of Los Angeles. "I've felt strong and independent. Like, I'm the boss of me." You go, Roni. That's exactly how you should feel.

If we, as women, don't embrace the positives of these experiences, guess what? We are as responsible as anyone else for perpetuating the old double standards associated with sleeping around—and that would be a shame. So, lest you feel even the slightest twinge of regret … lest you feel it's time to beat yourself up, rather than beat yourself off, we say you need to turn that frown upside down. And here's your step-by-step guide to doing just that.

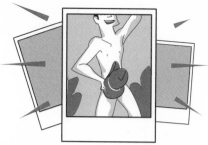

# Break Out the Souvenirs

We urge you to stop running away from the reminders of your night of passion and start looking upon them as a revival of sorts. What did you snag from his pad, if you went there? What did you take from the place where you met? If he offered his phone number, it's time to start that coitus collage! Oh, goodness, there are so many ways you can use the material possessions you've collected from the experience. If you followed the advice in the previous chapter about taking a Polaroid of each conquest, then you've got even more fuel for your mackdown memories.

# For the Record

We know journaling can be a sappy thing, and it's often for the wussiest of the women, but it can also be an incredibly cathartic way to get through a particular episode of your life. Not only that, but there is going to be a point in your life when you're no longer getting the sort of action you've been getting in these most triumphant single years . . . and trust us when we tell you that you are going to want to look back and remember these experiences, whether they were good, bad, or ugly. Time heals all wounds, so even if things went horribly wrong, there will be a day when you'll look back on it and laugh (or at least feel incredibly enlightened). Don't discount that, and don't allow yourself to forget these times. Write that shit down!

# *What Would Jesus Do?*

When it comes to the various perceptions of casual sex—particularly those of women who engage in it—we think good old J.C. said it best: "Judge not lest ye be judged." All we can do is give a big "amen" to that—and it might just be that no one's passing negative judgments on it anyway. For instance, check out what the guys who responded to our Happy Hook-Up survey say they think of a girl who has casual sex (for obvious reasons, of course . . . after all, they're getting some too, right?):

"I think she's independent and in control of her world."
 —*George, forty-six, Bethesda, Maryland*

"It's all good." —*Marty, thirty-four, Camden, New Jersey*

"I think it's great . . . especially when you can do it more than once."
 —*Johnny, thirty-four, Philadelphia*

"I have always considered it to be the best therapy known to mankind."
 —*Christopher, forty-seven, New York City*

"She's just as attractive as anyone else, but I don't necessarily need to hear all the details."
 —*Karl, twenty-two, Burbank, California*

"I applaud women who have casual sex . . . unless my hands are busy. "
 —*Chuck, thirty-four, Cleveland*

# Your Kiss Is on My List

Keeping a list of the guys you've screwed may seem horrifyingly pathetic or perverse. Guess what? It's not. It's actually one of the best things you can do for yourself . . . especially if there's any chance that something might go wrong after the fact. If you happen to contract an STD, you're going to want to know the who, what, when, where, why. (This is why we suggest getting his number.)

It's actually kind of fun to keep track, too. Think back to Andie MacDowell in *Four Weddings and a Funeral*: how cool was it when she and Hugh Grant were discussing previous conquests, and he asked her what "a good run" is these days? She listed off man after man that she'd done, characterizing each with at least a slight detail. Sure, she came mighty close to ruining the rest of the movie with her god-awful accent, but that list of been-there-done-hims made for a winning moment.

There's nothing wrong with keeping a list—it might actually be eye-opening and entertaining for you to do so. "I keep a list of the men with whom I've slept," says Carmen, twenty-six, of Portland, Maine. "For so many years, it was a tiny, tiny list, so I certainly didn't have to keep it written down. But when I had a bit of promiscuity, I got curious and started recording it. Then, a couple of years later, I'd actually forgotten the number, so I looked it all up and wrote the details down in a more official capacity." While Carmen admits that she's "compulsive and somewhat obsessed with [her] own history," we say it's an incredibly powerful and worthwhile pursuit. So, where's that pen?

## Why Aren't You Married Yet?

As a single woman, you're bound to encounter this question more than you'd care to—from friends, acquaintances, and at the dreaded family gatherings. That's why it's important to get into the casual-sex-celebration mind-set. The great thing is that if you've got a full and fulfilling sex life, you've got a very simple answer to this question: "I'm having too much fun having sex with a variety of men and can't make up my mind which one deserves me most." That ought to shut them up.

# Party Down

Look, you're not the only single girl in your crowd—and even if you are, the truth is that each and every one of you has probably had at least one casual sex encounter worth sharing. So, we suggest you all get together and bond over these moments—have an I-got-laid luau, if you will.

We threw a girls'-night-in party or two when we began researching this book. We not only invited over women we knew but told them to invite women they knew, and (just like in that old shampoo commercial) they told two friends, and they told two friends, and so on and so on. Eventually, it tuned into this incredibly cool gathering of upfront, adventurous, honest, empowered, fabulous females, who were laughing and talking, getting embarrassed or excited as they recalled their experiences. At the end of the night, not only had we all bonded—we'd learned a little bit more about each other and, more important, ourselves.

Women have actually thanked us for encouraging them to relive their casual sex days—they had never taken the time to consider what their views were, how they felt about their experiences, or the men, or anything beyond that. A Happy Hook-Up party can be so incredibly liberating and can bond you in new and amazing ways to the wonderful women out there. All you'll need are the following:

- An Invite: Encourage each woman to bring her stories and one bottle of wine.

- A Location: Any place will do. Simply kick out all the boys for the night.

- Name Tags: We suggest the standard "Hello, my name is _____," followed by, "and I've slept with [insert number] guys."

- Questionnaires: Either turn to appendix 1 and come up with a form that includes similar questions to the ones we've listed . . . or visit our website, happyhookup.com, and print out the questionnaires you find there. You'll be amazed at the stories it prompts and the laughter that ensues as your friends and fellow femme fatales respond to the questions and reminisce.

# No Regrets

When you get right down to it, you've got to realize that you had an enriching, perhaps even life-altering, experience, and there should be no lamenting it. "I've never really regretted having casual sex," says Kristin, thirty-nine, of Taos, New Mexico. "With some guys, it wasn't really worth it. I suppose they think now that I'm 'easy,' but I don't really care about that. Indeed. Screw that man, intellectually and emotionally, just as you did physically. What's done is done, and hopefully it was done well. If not, as we've said, learn from the experience and keep on truckin'.

# The Happy Hook-Up Survey Results

In doing research for this book we polled, quizzed, and hounded people—male and female, straight, gay, and bisexual—around the country for their views on and experiences with casual sex. They filled out questionnaires and surveys and gave them to us at our Happy Hook-Up research parties; via email; and via questionnaires they filled out at our website, happyhookup.com.

## Who Are These People?

Geographically, although a large percentage of the people who responded to our Happy Hook-Up surveys came from Los Angeles and New York, there were certainly a variety of other cities represented, from Baltimore to Wichita to Washington, D.C., to Atlanta.

The women who responded to our surveys and questionnaires were professionally diverse. They included students, financial advisors, environmental scientists, stylists, actresses, marketing directors, office managers, account executives, makeup artists, teachers, army officers, IT consultants, lab technicians, jewelry designers, writers, administrative assistants, bankers, sales representatives, copy editors, law students, web professionals, advertising executives, training specialists, entrepreneurs, journalists, designers, speech pathologists, producers, and publicists. They ranged in age from nineteen to forty-seven years old.

The men who responded to our surveys and questionnaires weren't quite as diverse but included actors, writers, directors, musicians, marketing executives, furniture designers, technology managers, engineers, record executives, policy analysts, therapists, and geologists, and ranged in age from twenty-four to forty-nine years old.

# What Did They Say?

From how many people they've had casual sex with, to how they define it, to what causes them to become emotionally attached, here's what the respondents reported:

## Questionnaire Number 1:
## Everybody Has Their Own Opinion

*The women weigh in with theirs*

What's your definition of casual sex?

- "Commitment-free, 'sperm-of-the-moment' intercourse."

- "Sex with someone that you're not dating exclusively."

- "Casual intercourse or oral sex leading to fluid exchange."

- "Casual sex equals anytime, anywhere. Usually happens on an evening when a lot of booze has been consumed."

- "Sex with someone with whom you have not been out on adate. You've simply hung out in a group setting or met in a social situation."

- "Sex is never casual for me, so even if I have sex just once with someone, it's a powerful experience that I wouldn't define as casual. Casual implies indifference. I am never indifferent when I have sex. I'm an active participant open to the experience physically and emotionally."

- "Plain and simple: sex without commitment."

- "The act of playing around just for fun in the moment. There's no commitment, no relationship."

- "Sex without a deep kind of love and admiration."

What's your opinion of women who have casual sex?

- "If they are emotionally strong enough to not feel dirty or rejected by it, I am proud of their sexual independence. If they later feel ashamed or cheap, I think they are suckers."

- "I have no judgment against women who have casual sex. The important things are to play safe and not do anything (or anyone) you don't want to do."

- "I sort of feel sorry for them because I know why I used to partake in it—because I had no monogamous prospects and, while it felt good, it was mostly instant gratification, and I just wanted to feel good and appear sexy to the person I was sleeping with. I secretly hoped they would want to be with me always."

- "Go on, girls!"

- "Good for them. As long as they are clear about what they want (and honest with themselves about their reasons for doing it), then more power to them."

- "They're my favorite people."

- "There's nothing wrong with it—in moderation."

- "Depends on the reason, I suppose, why they're engaging in casual sex. Mostly, I think they're courageous and probably just exploring who they are. They aren't afraid to go against the grain."

- "It depends on their motives. I think women who can enjoy sex and have a casual attitude about it are healthy and great. I think women who try to make sex into a relationship when no other basis for it exists, or women who have sex always thinking it will lead to something else, are a little sad."

- "Who am I to judge? I've been around that block more than I can remember."

- "As I get older, I feel that women who *choose* to have casual sex are empowered. There's a lot of freedom in consciously deciding to have casual sex and to not be attached to someone."

What's your opinion of men who have casual sex?

- "I guess I approve, but I don't think it is acceptable for men to discuss the encounter with their friends. I don't approve when men judge women for the same actions. I also don't like it when men take advantage of women who clearly don't know that it is casual. And I don't like men who think that they were able to have sex because they (the men) were special and the women must really like them. Not true."

- "I think it's perfectly fine, as long as they protect themselves against the nasties out there and don't tell women they love them or they'll call them or make false promises of any kind. If you just want to get laid, say so. We are big girls and that's probably all we wanted anyway."

- "Go on, boys . . . but realize you're never going to satisfy us. You think you're doing it to women, but women are doing it to *you*. Ha ha."

- "Are there any that don't?"

- "Same as women—nothing wrong with it unless they're doing it every weekend. Then the risk factor gets too high."
- "I just think they're looking for an evening of enjoyment rather than a relationship."

What evidence, if any, have you seen of a double standard when it comes to women and men who have casual sex?

- "The three-date rule and the fact that men don't respect women who sleep with them on the first date or first meeting. I've had many relationships develop from one-night stands, but there is still a stigma if a girl sleeps with a guy too soon."
- "I definitely think women tend to be judged for having casual sex, while men are congratulated for it."
- "It's improved through the years, but women still get labeled as 'sluts' or 'loose,' when the men are considered players."
- "Men still call women 'sluts.' Sure, women call men 'players,' but how is that bad? Women are still given derogatory names, while men aren't."
- "People assume that the woman is more serious than the guy, when that may not be the case. (Like, 'Oh, poor Carolyn. She has no idea that he has a girlfriend. She's going to get her heart broken.' How do you know Carolyn doesn't have a boyfriend? What makes you think she's more into him than he is into her?)"
- "For one thing, I've had discussions with men who admit they don't want a serious relationship or marriage with a woman who's slept around a lot. Also, I once dated a man who got pushy for sex a little soon. I slept with him after dating for a week (we had seen each other every night). After a few times of sleeping together, he backed way off. He told me that a friend of his told him: "If she'd have sex with you that quickly, she'd sleep with

anybody"—the thrust (pardon the pun) being that I was too easy and possibly a risky partner and he therefore lost interest."

- "The obvious: men are glorified for casual sex; women are normally looked upon as easy."

- "People view women who have casual sex as either easy or as having low self-esteem, while men are viewed as studs if they have casual sex."

- "Men are heroes—women are whores."

- "Men want to date women who have casual sex, but they want to marry virgins."

At what point, if any, do you become emotionally attached to someone with whom you're having/have had casual sex and why?

- "I become emotionally attached if I know the guy well and want him for more than just sex . . . so, if that's the case, I become emotionally attached even before we have sex."

- "I am emotionally attached to just about everyone. If I have sex with someone I don't know, I have a kick-ass high and then usually wish I hadn't. It is such an intimate activity. If I can't or don't want to see that person again, after being physically attached, I feel lonely and bad about it."

- "A few times, I've thought I could have casual sex without becoming attached, but I usually can't—especially if it's more than a one-night stand. I think I become attached as I spend more time with the man. If, while naked in his arms in bed, you can feel comfortable and sexy and laugh and talk, how can you not start to fall for him? Why wouldn't you want him to be part of your life? The problem is that men can have a great time with you in bed, and laugh and talk and really enjoy the whole experience of being with you, beyond the sex, then walk out the door and not look back. Or if they are looking back, they manage to do it without being moved to see you again."

- "There's always a certain amount of attachment after sleeping with someone, if for nothing else than to want to continue having sex with him."

What are/would be your reasons for having casual sex?

- "Casual sex allows you to be selfish and not feel guilty. You have no responsibilities and no attachments to this person."
- "Casual sex is a great way to get over a breakup."
- "I have casual sex with someone when I'm attracted to him physically but not emotionally."
- "I've had casual sex when there hasn't been a man in my life for a long time, and I'm starting to get lonely—and horny!"
- "For fun. Why not, as long as I don't have deeper feelings for the person?"
- "I enjoy sex and if I am not in a relationship and have a mutual attraction with someone, I'll probably follow it through."
- "Horny."
- "Horny."
- "Horny."
- "Pure physical pleasure."
- "Intense attraction, horniness."
- "It's fun. I'm horny. I don't have a boyfriend at the time. My boyfriend isn't around at the time!"
- "It's an ego boost. It makes me feel sexy and attractive."
- "Rebound. Proving I don't need someone as much as I might. Trying something/someone new. Curiosity."

- "Physical intimacy. Sometimes it's easier to be less inhibited with someone you don't know well."

What do you view as the advantages to having casual sex rather than having a serious relationship, if any?

- "Sometimes you just want a one-night stand. No dealing with living with someone, baggage, bullshit, etc."

- "It lets you get to know the most intimate parts of someone else before making a commitment. It's spontaneous; it can be a great way to have physical contact with another human being when you're not ready for the emotional baggage."

- "A committed relationship requires enormous energy and sacrifice. For me, personally, being part of a couple is not appealing for many reasons."

- "I will have sex with someone who I know is inappropriate for me in a larger sense: men who are too young or don't have a job or drink too much; or even a woman. They are attractive, but not desirable for a long-term thing."

- "You can have multiple partners, no strings; you don't have to answer to anyone else."

- "The ability to date openly; he does his thing, I do mine; no guilt over other casual sex experiences."

- "It's better to not be in a relationship with anyone, and be able to have a little fun now and then, than it is to be involved with the wrong person."

- "There are a lot of advantages to having casual sex. It's a great way to gain knowledge about what you're looking for in a guy. It's also a great way to learn about sex, men, and your own body, so you know what the hell you're doing when you get with the person with whom you may want a serious relationship."

- "If you just want to get off, rather than deal with a relationship, casual sex is the way to go. Sometimes the sex is good, but you know the guy would probably be useless as a boyfriend."

- "If those involved understand the terms of the sex, casual sex can be much more uninhibited (with the emotional aspects removed). It becomes purely about physical pleasure."

- "One, getting a need met with out having to hear the man talk about himself all night. Two, the freedom to ask for what I really want without feeling shame or judgment. Three, selfish stress relief without having to hear about someone else's day or pretending to care about his issues."

- "No bullshit. No annoying emotional entanglements. No expectations."

- "If there is an understanding that it is what it is, and both people are mature enough to separate the issues of companionship and romance, then it's great. The important thing is that both parties are honest, and one doesn't secretly harbor fantasies that it could turn into something more."

What do you view as the disadvantages to having casual sex, rather than having a serious relationship, if any?

- "If, once you do have sex, you get attached and the other person isn't interested in a serious relationship, it can be depressing."

- "Sometimes, someone's feelings can get hurt. Sometimes, someone can get an STD."

- "Sticky situations, STDs. If you're not emotionally ready, it can lead to a full mental meltdown."

- "When you partake in it for the wrong reasons, you run the risk of being deluded all the time and not investing time and effort into building a real relationship."

- "It is obviously dangerous. The guy may have a disease or be a psycho. In addition to that, sometimes you just want to kiss someone you like more than just sexually, and it can start to feel kind of empty."

- "You feel a wee bit empty afterwards . . . like, why doesn't he want me for more than that—and why don't I want *him* for more than that?"

- "You don't get to a deep level of intimacy. You don't get someone to snuggle with on rainy days, or go to the grocery store or plan to buy a house with. You're still technically alone."

- "Ultimately, I want that house in the suburbs with 2.5 kids. Actually maybe one kid and lots of dogs."

What do you do to plan ahead for casual sex, if anything?

- "When I was single, I used to plan, strategize—the whole thing! Shaving, buffing, polishing, cleaning the house and bedroom, preparing everything in general, so that it all came off as uncontrived as possible when the guy actually was in the bedroom. The point was to make everything seem as effortless as possible —to show him: "See how fab I am, and I don't even try?!" Of course, this was dumb and, ninety percent of the time, a waste of energy because they didn't notice or appreciate it anyway!"

- "I always carry condoms, never expect a phone call, wear easy-access clothes, carry some makeup with me for the morning after—and I try to always have my own car with me for a fast getaway."

- "I have condoms. I wear sexy underwear. I shave my legs. If it's a big plan (for instance, if I have a recurring friend visiting from out of town), I get a bikini wax. I wear lotions and oils. Just your basic, sexy, personal hygiene stuff."

- "I have planned to have casual sex with someone I already know. I dress up. I plan on having fun. Of course, those are usually the times I don't have it. Casual sex always seems to happen out of the blue."

- "I have protection. I get the house ready with candles and such."

- "A few times, I've totally not expected to take someone home when I did. And a couple of times, I'd be in the mood, or have been running into some hot guy every week at a bar, and decided I would go for it. So to get ready, I, of course, get condoms, straighten up my messy apartment, and make sure to shave my legs."

- "I do the usual 'yard work' (shaving, bleaching, whatever else needs doing). I have condoms at home, and I might carry them with me. I make sure that I'm not wearing anything that would kill it (undies with holes, stinky shoes, support hose)."

How have your views on casual sex changed as you've grown older, if at all?

- "I think I've become more comfortable with the idea of casual sex; I know who I am with or without a relationship, so I also feel more comfortable with casual sex."

- "I used to think only easy, slutty women had casual sex, and that I never could. Now, I know that it's part of my pure, sexual power ...that I am invincible...that I can have sex with whomever I like...if I weren't married, of course!"

- "I think when we're younger, casual sex tends to occur for the wrong reasons—especially for females. Insecurity, fear, needing acceptance, all play a role. But as we get older, I think it tends to be more of a choice and the motivation changes."

- "I was a 'good girl' all my life. As I approached my forties, as a divorced, single woman with a *growing* sex drive, I felt the need to own my sexuality, instead of letting it own me."

- "Let's just say, in high school, I wanted to save myself for marriage, and five years later, I have slept with over ten people, and some of those, I never knew their names."

- "I think I needed a period of promiscuity in my life. But I was older when I did it—like thirty. I had a much better sense of myself. I almost felt it was something I'd like to get out of my system—that it would be a good learning experience for me. It really was. I learned a lot about what I liked and disliked in men, not just sexually, but about them as people. That helped me in future relationships."

## Questionnaire Number 2: The Boys' Club

*The men offer up their opinions*

What's your best advice to women for becoming emotionally detached, or not wanting more from a guy after casual sex?

- "Don't do it for all the wrong reasons. Just because it's casual sex doesn't mean it's not discriminating. If you're becoming too emotional or totally detached, I would advise you to give it a rest for a bit."

- "Think about it before you do it. And enjoy!"

- "Focus on things that she can achieve in her life. Let the casual sex be filed with the recreational things we do to round out our lives."

- "Don't think of the act as 'love making'—consider it solving a problem or taking care of some business."

- "Enjoy that ability to have sex and not feel guilty about it."

- "Don't have it."
- "Call me the next time you're horny!"

How are you (or guys you know) able to have casual sex without becoming emotionally attached?

- "I'm thinking about the four or five other girls that I know that I also want to have sex with."
- "I get together with someone who has a few issues that keep me from considering her a long-term option, e.g., she's really flaky, so I couldn't stand dealing with her as a girlfriend, but as an occasional hookup, sure."
- "Some men can separate sex from emotion, especially if it's not with a woman who you spend a lot of time with. It's easier when we are younger too."
- "Men: two heads, no brain in either one."
- "Men are designed to have as many kids as possible, to keep the species varied and kickin'. Women are designed to become very attached emotionally to men in order to ensure that they take child rearing seriously. A woman might not love a child as much if it's sired without love involved. Men don't have this problem. We have a big part of our brains that's closed down with a sign hanging that reads, "I quit giving a shit about this kinda stuff twenty thousand years ago.""

What do you think of a girl who's prepared for casual sex (e.g. has condoms, seems ready for action, etc.)?

- "Good for her!"
- "She's smarter and more on top of her game than a girl who is 'winging it' and not paying attention to important details like health."

- "Knows what she wants and is willing to be safe about it. Good plan."
- "Thank goodness—it shows she cares about herself, and if she does sleep around, she doesn't want to die doing it."
- "Great."
- "I think she's smart."
- "Very intelligent."
- "*Not* showing up with protection is offensive."

In what instances, if any, would you ask for the phone number of someone with whom you've had casual sex?

- "If I was still interested in either another hook-up or potentially a longer relationship."
- "If it was really good and I thought it could happen again, of course."
- "If I had a good time and it seemed they had one as well."

Do you generally (or ever) want to see—or have a relationship with—someone with whom you've had casual sex? Why or why not?

- "Half the time, I'm open to more dating and more sex. A few times, I want one more hook-up with this woman for good sex, but I can tell already that she won't be a good fit with most of my regular world."
- "No. Come on."
- "I'm no hater. I wouldn't want to sleep with a woman I didn't want to hang with. That's just weird."
- "Yes. It's happened before. It was casual sex that saved my sanity."

# Questionnaire Number 3:
# Bedtime Stories from Boys and Girls

*More sexcapades from the casual sex trenches*

What was your best casual sex encounter?

THE GIRLS:

- "Driving back from a party in San Luis Obispo, I was giving a guy I had just met a ride home. We started touching each other in the car, and just got so damn horny, we pulled over at a park, brought out a blanket, and did it under an oak tree."

- "I was at a beach rave on Nantucket, and the cops broke it up. My girlfriends and I ran away down the shore (they with the men they'd just met, me alone). After hiding around a bend in the shoreline, I decided to go back to the car, when a man with a strong accent said to me, "No. Policia!" and then told me my hair looked so beautiful in the moonlight. I knew it was all over for me. We walked further down the shore and had sex right there in the moonlight, with occasional sirens and flashing lights."

- "With a friend who had been very shy and quiet in person, while we were working on a performance project, but who several weeks later emailed me a dream he had had that included me. This sparked two weeks of innuendo-driven emails back and forth, until finally he came to see the current show I was appearing in. We went back to his place afterwards and talked for two hours with our faces just inches apart, until finally I gave in and kissed him, and it all snowballed from there. He was fantastic. The shy ones always get me."

- "Oh, with a crush! We had sex at his condo in Malibu overlooking the ocean. Sigh."

- "It was when I was in high school, fooling around in the basement of the school with a boy I had a crush on. It was so hot because it was the first time I was ever touched by another person. Those first sensations are always the best."

- "I've had four casual sex encounters over the years, and none of them were good."

THE BOYS:

- "A tie. A sex-crazed chorus girl in a show I directed who had a bookshelf that consisted only of two things: Babar books and Anaïs Nin novels. (This is a signal that says: Screwball! Daddy issues! Full speed ahead!) I remember vividly coming on her perfectly washboard-like stomach after pulling out. A close second would be a girl I directed in a Disney pageant: enormously tall with beautiful feet like little cream cheeses. A perfectly gorgeous, bland, dimwitted Orange County future homemaker and soccer mom, perverted before her time."

- "While in my freshman year of college in Boston, we had a game called 'Goddess of the Week.' I was a virgin at the time. During that week, if the selected individual communicated or committed any kind of act, you received points. For example, if she said 'Hi' to you, that was 1 point; 'How are you' got two points. If she speaks your name, that was five, etc. No one had any real points by the end of the year, so the game ended.

  "Four years later, I bumped into one of the former goddesses of the week. She was extremely sexy. She and I got to talking, and the conversation headed to a nostalgic look at our past. She let me know that she always wanted to sleep with me but didn't want to be my first. I let her know that I had had some experience since the old days, and she immediately declared that she wanted to sleep with me. We went directly to her place. The room was set for passion: hers!

"Netting hung from the ceiling and draped over the bed, candles everywhere, and the smell of incense filled the air. It was evening, and we started with some tender kisses, followed by very sensual touching, then licking, etc. It went on for hours, with taunting and teasing and aggression. It was all too erotic.

"The next morning after I left—and agreeing to do it again—I called my friend from freshman year inquiring as to how many points I would get for sleeping with her. 'You win,' he said."

- "Checking into a hotel in Texas. A girl was trying to get the electronic key in the slot. I opened her door and she gave me a kiss on the cheek to thank me. Thirty seconds later our clothes were off and I was banging her against the balcony overlooking the pool. She said she would stop by my room the next night with her sister. I never saw her again."

What was your funniest casual sex encounter?

THE GIRLS:

- "Doing it in a storage room at a bar and someone walking in on us. Oops!"

- "In high school, giving a blow job in the balcony of the auditorium while a rehearsal for *Damn Yankees* was taking place on stage."

- "I took this guy home from a bar with me only to find out on the way home that he was twenty. The next morning, he saw a picture of my nephew on my bedside table and asked if I had a kid. Because I was twenty-eight, he assumed that being that old, I must have children."

THE BOYS:

- "Sleeping with someone while having a Catholic Church service playing on the radio."

- "My car alarm going off in the parking lot of the Palm. All the valets ran over to check out a girl I had just had my first date with, on top of me. They didn't charge me for parking that night. True story."

What was your most embarrassing casual sex encounter?

THE GIRLS:

- "I flatulated during oral. Can you imagine?"

- "Fooling around with two guys in a port-a-potty at our school carnival. When the three of us walked out, there were little kids and their parents waiting to use the bathroom. Talk about disgusting and embarrassing!"

- "It was early winter. I hooked up with a guy from work. We started making out, and he began to undress me. I had forgot to shave my legs, and they were really hairy. We had sex, and he was thrusting so hard, I was afraid he would tear me! Later, we were both trying to fall asleep. Then he starts trying to have sex with me again. The second time, he did not put on a condom. I was about to say something, but he pulled out and started jerking off! I didn't know what to do, so I just hid my face. Why did he have to jerk off in front of me? Ahhh!"

THE BOYS:
*Authors' note: The men we polled couldn't bring themselves to admit to ever having an embarrassing encounter . . . go figure!*

What was your most disappointing casual sex encounter?

THE GIRLS:

- "I was on the rebound on Halloween and all dolled up as a mermaid. I had sex with a man dressed as a 'dyke': fake, sagging boobs in a white wife-beater shirt, and dorky glasses.

Unfortunately, he was much hotter as a lesbian than a man, and reminded me far too much of the man I was rebounding from."

- "A guy who was surprisingly ultra-hairy once I got his clothes off. Yuck."

- "It was someone I had a huge crush on, but when he finally made the move, he wasn't hard. So rather than thinking about it, I said out loud, "Is it *in*?" We had sex only one time, one year later."

- "Making out with a guy on my bed (trying to take things 'slow'), only to find him pulling his dick out uninvited, jerking off, leaving a puddle of cum on my bedspread, and soon after walking out the door."

- "All of them. I think each guy was trying to prove something— be Mr. Fantastic Lover. The sex was hard sex. I never climaxed with any of them."

THE BOYS:

- "Starting to mess around with a woman who had a bad urine smell. I tried to fake it, but couldn't, so I got out of there."

- "During an encounter, I cut my mouth while sucking her toes. I got four stitches and couldn't think of a lie to tell the resident, so I told the truth."

- "I met an adorable girl through a friend, and we went out to some Hollywood rock show. We had drinks and got frisky. Back at her place, it became clear just what effect the drinks had had on her—after she rather incoherently demanded to be tied up (a request I satisfied by clumsily joining her hands with her shirt), she rather brusquely slurred her insistence that we jump right to the main event. Preferring to engage in foreplay first, I began going down on her. The effect of my ministrations was quickly made manifest: she was not only unconscious but *snoring*."

What was your weirdest casual sex encounter?

THE GIRLS:

- "At an art gallery opening, I gave a blow job to a guy in the elevator. We just kept going up and down."

- "Meeting some guy at a bar when I was wasted and going back to his apartment. He got me completely naked on his couch, and I realized that I didn't even know his name or if he was a raving lunatic."

- "I was at a club in Houston one night, and I ended up having sex with the lead singer of this band that performed. We did it in the band's tour van. I looked up and saw a video camera and turned over to get doggy style. When I did, I saw my best friend screwing the drummer in the back of the van, right next to me. She and I were face-to-face in the same position!"

THE BOYS:

*Authors' note: And, when it comes to casual sex, few things are weird or shocking to the men we polled.*

What was your worst morning-after or walk-of-shame experience?

THE GIRLS:

- "Being dropped off at 7 A.M. after a night of debauchery, still in my waitress uniform, only to find my dad in the living room working on the computer. I just said, 'Don't ask,' and he replied, 'I won't.'"

- "When I slept with this guy, and we were screaming and wailing with pleasure at the top of our lungs. The next morning as I headed to the bathroom, I ran into his mother. She'd heard the whole thing—I could tell from how she looked at me."

- "It was more like the 'drive of shame.' I was heading home early one morning with a terrible hangover, when I got into a car accident. I had just gone out on a date and had casual sex with a new guy. The impact of the accident was hard enough to pop the zipper on the front of my dress (it went all the way down the dress). Since this happened just outside my old boyfriend and first love's apartment, I realized it would probably be a good idea to just go in and ask him to help me. At first, he was mad that he had to deal with his crying ex-girlfriend—standing there in a split dress with a jacket wrapped around me. Oddly enough, his anger soon subsided and turned to excitement as he watched me standing there in what was basically my underwear. He decided he wanted to have sex with me, and off we went to his place. The ironic part is that one of the reasons I had gone out on a date the night before was to get over him."

THE BOYS:

- "Being with an Afghan woman who had terrible morning-after angst. Let me tell you, twenty-first century people: whatever you think Catholic guilt is or Jewish guilt is, multiply it by something like a jillion and that's Muslim guilt."

# The Happy Hook-Up Survey

How many people have you had casual sex with (ballpark)?

|  | WOMEN | MEN |
|---|---|---|
| 0: | 6 percent | 0 percent |
| 1–5: | 17 percent | 16 percent |
| 6–10: | 29 percent | 16 percent |
| 11–plus: | 48 percent | 68 percent |

How many of those people were same-sex encounters?

|  | WOMEN | MEN |
|---|---|---|
| 0: | 84 percent | 85 percent |
| 1–5: | 15 percent | 5 percent |
| 6–10: | 0 percent | 5 percent |
| 11–plus: | 1 percent | 5 percent |

How many times have you had group casual sex
(three or more people total)?

|  | WOMEN | MEN |
|---|---|---|
| 0: | 81 percent | 63 percent |
| 1–5: | 17 percent | 37 percent |
| 6–10: | 2 percent | 0 percent |
| 11–plus: | 0 percent | 0 percent |

Did you lose your virginity in a casual sex encounter?

|  | WOMEN | MEN |
|---|---|---|
| Yes: | 22 percent | 53 percent |
| No: | 78 percent | 47 percent |

## How many times have you had casual sex while sober?

|  | WOMEN | MEN |
|---|---|---|
| 0: | 30 percent | 11 percent |
| 1–5: | 39 percent | 16 percent |
| 6–10: | 15 percent | 16 percent |
| 11–plus: | 16 percent | 57 percent |

## How many times have you had casual sex without using condoms?

|  | WOMEN | MEN |
|---|---|---|
| 0: | 29 percent | 16 percent |
| 1–5: | 38 percent | 36 percent |
| 6–10: | 18 percent | 11 percent |
| 11–plus: | 15 percent | 37 percent |

## How many times has casual sex led to a serious relationship for you?

|  | WOMEN | MEN |
|---|---|---|
| 0: | 45 percent | 42 percent |
| 1–5: | 48 percent | 47 percent |
| 6–10: | 7 percent | 11 percent |
| 11–plus: | 0 percent | 0 percent |

## How many exes have you gone back to for one last time?

|  | WOMEN | MEN |
|---|---|---|
| 0: | 31 percent | 31 percent |
| 1–5: | 57 percent | 53 percent |
| 6–10: | 6 percent | 5 percent |
| 11–plus: | 6 percent | 11 percent |

## What's the fastest you've ever had casual sex with someone you just met?

|  | WOMEN | MEN |
|---|---|---|
| Within minutes: | 13 percent | 6 percent |
| Within hours: | 69 percent | 89 percent |
| Within days: | 10 percent | 5 percent |
| Within a week: | 8 percent | 0 percent |

## Do you generally give your phone number to someone with whom you've had casual sex?

|  | WOMEN | MEN |
|---|---|---|
| Yes: | 67 percent | 95 percent |
| No: | 33 percent | 5 percent |

## Do you generally ask for/take the number of someone with whom you've had casual sex?

|  | WOMEN | MEN |
|---|---|---|
| Yes: | 42 percent | 89 percent |
| No: | 58 percent | 11 percent |

## Do you generally hope you'll hear from someone with whom you've had casual sex or see them again?

|  | WOMEN | MEN |
|---|---|---|
| Yes: | 57 percent | 47 percent |
| No: | 43 percent | 53 percent |

## Do you think it's necessary to make it clear to each other that this is just casual sex before, during, or after having it?

|  | WOMEN | MEN |
|---|---|---|
| Yes: | 36 percent | 53 percent |
| No: | 64 percent | 47 percent |

## Do you generally spend the whole night with someone with whom you've had casual sex?

|         | WOMEN      | MEN        |
|---------|------------|------------|
| Yes:    | 69 percent | 63 percent |
| No:     | 31 percent | 37 percent |

## How do you generally feel about yourself after having casual sex?

|                  | WOMEN      | MEN        |
|------------------|------------|------------|
| Empowered:       | 11 percent | 11 percent |
| Guilty:          | 16 percent | 11 percent |
| Sexy/Attractive: | 29 percent | 32 percent |
| Depressed:       | 3 percent  | 10 percent |
| Other:           | 41 percent | 36 percent |

## Have you ever regretted having casual sex?

|         | WOMEN      | MEN        |
|---------|------------|------------|
| Yes:    | 87 percent | 95 percent |
| No:     | 13 percent | 5 percent  |

## Have you ever had casual sex with someone your friend(s) didn't approve of?

|         | WOMEN      | MEN        |
|---------|------------|------------|
| Yes:    | 70 percent | 74 percent |
| No:     | 30 percent | 26 percent |

## Would you rather have casual sex with someone who is:

|                                   | WOMEN      | MEN        |
|-----------------------------------|------------|------------|
| Smart:                            | 12 percent | 0 percent  |
| Sensitive:                        | 5 percent  | 0 percent  |
| Attractive:                       | 34 percent | 68 percent |
| Well endowed/ sexually skilled:   | 49 percent | 32 percent |

# Fun with STDs

s we told you in chapter 2, the more sexual partners you have, the better your odds of contracting a disease—and there are more than twenty-five diseases or infections (STDs or STIs) spread primarily by sexual activity. Thus, before we end this book, we feel we must fill you in on some of the biggies. We consulted a variety of expert resources, including the Centers for Disease Control and Prevention (CDC), National Institutes of Health (NIH), the American Social Health Association (ASHA), and the Sexuality Information and Education Council of the United States (SIECUS) to bring you the following details. That said, we cannot guarantee the absolute accuracy of this information, and therefore encourage you to talk to your doctor or contact the CDC National STD Hotline at (800) 227-8922 or (800) 342-2437 for the most reliable, comprehensive, up-to-date facts.

## Bacterial Vaginosis (BV)

There's not a whole lot known about this STD, but essentially your vagina has lots of "good" bacteria in it and some "harmful" bacteria. BV develops when the harmful stuff increases—which can happen to any woman, but women with a new sex partner or multiple sex partners (male or female), women who douche, and those who use an intrauterine device (IUD) for contraception are at greater risk. Although BV will sometimes clear up without treatment, all women with symptoms should be treated to avoid such complications as pelvic inflammatory disease (PID; see below), one of the most common causes of infertility. BV can also increase your susceptibility to other STDs, such as HIV, chlamydia, and gonorrhea. The symptoms can include an abnormal white or gray vaginal discharge that may be thin and may have an unpleasant odor (often strong and fish-like, particularly after intercourse). You may also experience burning during urination, itching around the outside of the vagina, or both. However, some women with BV report no symptoms at all. Male partners generally don't need to be treated.

## Chlamydia

Chlamydia is a tricky little disease that can be transmitted during vaginal, anal, or oral sex. Since about 75 percent of infected women and 50 percent of infected men have no symptoms, you probably won't even know you have it. An estimated 2.8 million Americans are infected each year—but the most recent number of annual cases reported to the CDC was just over 830,000. If you do have symptoms, they may include abnormal vaginal discharge or a burning sensation when you urinate. On the upside, if you catch it early, a dose of antibiotics will get rid of it. Left untreated, it can lead to PID (see below).

## Genital Herpes

Herpes is an extremely common STD in America, affecting an estimated forty-five million people. It is an incurable viral infection caused by herpes simplex viruses HSV-1 and HSV-2 and is transmitted through skin-to-skin contact during unprotected anal, oral, or vaginal sex with an infected person or through kissing. Individuals are often not aware they are infected with herpes because there are either no symptoms, mild symptoms, or symptoms that are mistaken for other health problems such as yeast infections, insect bites, or hemorrhoids. HSV-1 can cause genital herpes but more often infects the mouth and lips, causing cold sores or fever blisters. HSV-2 is generally contracted via sexual contact with someone who has it whether they have a visible sore or not. Painful blisters or open sores may appear within days of contracting herpes, but may not appear for weeks, months, or years. Although sores usually disappear within two to three weeks, the virus stays with you like a bad hangover (one that lasts for life, though), and can recur from time to time. Severe recurrences can be treated with one of several prescription drugs, but you'll never be completely cured.

## Gonorrhea

Also known as "the clap," this is another common STD in the States, with approximately 700,000 new cases annually (though only half of those are reported to the CDC each year). It is spread through contact between the penis, vagina, mouth, and anus, and nobody's got to ejaculate for it to be transmitted or acquired. Again, because symptoms tend to be mild, women often don't know they have it, and sometimes mistake it for a bladder infection. The initial symptoms and signs in women include a painful or burning sensation when urinating, increased vaginal discharge, or vaginal bleeding between periods. The most common and serious complications occur in women and, as with chlamydia, these include PID. Several antibiotics can successfully treat gonorrhea, and because many people with gonorrhea also have chlamydia, antibiotics for both infections are usually given together. If you have gonorrhea, be sure to get tested for other STDs.

## Hepatitis B (HBV)

This is the only STD for which a vaccine is available. The virus causes chronic infection, cirrhosis (scarring), and cancer of the liver and is transmitted through unprotected anal, vaginal, or oral sex with an infected person. Using condoms may reduce transmission. If you're at risk for HBV infection, you might also be at risk for infection with Hepatitis C or HIV. About 30 percent of infected people have no signs or symptoms, but if you do have symptoms, they'll include jaundice, fatigue, abdominal pain, loss of appetite, nausea, vomiting, or joint pain. Death from chronic liver disease occurs in 15 to 25 percent of chronically infected persons.

## Human Immunodeficiency Virus (HIV)

This virus destroys the body's ability to fight off infections and cancers. After developing a number of these infections or reaching a certain blood count level, an HIV-positive person is diagnosed with Acquired Immunodeficiency Syndrome (AIDS). HIV is present in blood, semen, vaginal secretions, and breast milk. Transmission primarily occurs during sexual activity and by sharing needles used to inject intravenous drugs. Nearly one million Americans are currently infected with HIV. The only way to know if you're infected is to be tested for it, particularly since symptoms may not manifest at all for many years. That said, if exposed to HIV you still may not test positive for three to six months, so if you feel you're at risk you should be tested periodically. People who have HIV and AIDS are highly susceptible to many life-threatening diseases and certain forms of cancer. From 1998 through 2002, the number of AIDS diagnoses increased 7 percent among women. Heterosexual contact is now the greatest risk for women; sex with drug users plays a large role. In 2000, 38 percent of women with AIDS were infected through heterosexual exposure to HIV; injection drug use accounted for 25 percent of cases.

## Human Papillomavirus (HPV)

There are more than one hundred different strains or types of this viral STD and more than thirty of them are sexually transmitted, infecting the skin of the penis, vulva, or anus, and the linings of the vagina, cervix, or rectum. Once again, you probably won't have any symptoms. HPV is transmitted by direct skin-to-skin contact with an infected individual; infection can occur even when condoms protect the affected areas, although condom use has been associated with a lower rate of cervical cancer, an HPV-associated disease. It can take weeks, months, or years to manifest. Men who have been exposed to the strains that affect the cervix can contract the virus, and while it doesn't affect them (since they don't have a cervix), they can pass the virus to other women without knowing it. The good news is that the majority of infections eventually go away on their own—but it's important to monitor the condition by getting regular Paps. "High-risk" types of HPV can cause abnormal Pap tests and may lead to cancer of the cervix, vulva, vagina, anus, or penis. Others are called "low-risk" types, and they may cause mild Pap test abnormalities or genital warts. (Genital warts are bumps that appear in the genital area and can be treated topically or surgically removed. Warts may appear within weeks or months of contact with an infected person, or not at all.) Approximately 20 million people are currently infected with HPV and 6.2 million Americans get a new genital HPV infection each year.

## Pelvic Inflammatory Disease (PID)

This is a common complication of some STDs, especially chlamydia and gonorrhea. It can damage the fallopian tubes and tissues in and near the uterus and ovaries and, left untreated, can lead to infertility, ectopic pregnancy (a pregnancy in the fallopian tube or elsewhere outside of the womb), abscess formation, and chronic pelvic pain. It is estimated that more than one million women experience an episode of acute PID and more than 100,000 women become infertile each year as a result of PID. Women who douche or who use IUDs may have a higher risk of developing PID. While signs or symptoms can be absent or mild, they may include fever, unusual vaginal discharge that may have a foul odor, painful intercourse, painful urination, irregular menstrual bleeding, and, in rare cases, pain in the right upper abdomen. PID can be cured with several types of antibiotics, but medication does not reverse any damage that has already occurred to the reproductive organs.

## Pubic Lice (pediculosis pubis or crab lice)

These are tiny critters that generally hang out in your pubic hair and survive by sucking human blood. Condoms won't protect you since you can catch them by rubbing yourself against someone who's infected, or even via contact with infested bedding or clothing. An estimated three million people with new cases of the infestation are treated each year in the United States.

## Scabies

A skin infestation with a tiny mite that's highly contagious and is spread the same way as crabs. It's occasionally confused with other skin irritations, such as poison ivy or eczema.

## Syphilis

Syphilis has often been called "the great imitator" because so many of the signs and symptoms are similar to those of other diseases. The initial symptom is a painless open sore that usually appears on the penis or around or in the vagina, near the mouth, anus, or on the hands. It's passed from person to person through direct contact with a sore during vaginal, anal, or oral sex. However, many people don't have any symptoms for years, or don't recognize the sores, so oftentimes the disease is transmitted by people who don't know they're infected. Penicillin or other antibiotics are available to treat syphilis—but if you don't get screened and it goes unnoticed, syphilis may go on to more advanced stages, including a rash and, eventually, serious involvement of the heart and central nervous system. In the United States, health officials reported over 32,000 cases of syphilis in 2002.

### Trichomoniasis (or "trich")

This is caused by a parasite and is the most prevalent curable STD in young sexually active women. An estimated 7.4 million new cases occur each year in women and men. The vagina is the most common site of infection in women, and the urethra is the most common site of infection in men. The parasite is transmitted through penis-to-vagina intercourse or vulva-to-vulva contact. Women can acquire the disease from infected men or women, but men usually contract it only from infected women. Signs or symptoms of infection in women may include a frothy, yellow-green vaginal discharge with a strong odor. The infection also may cause discomfort during intercourse and urination, as well as irritation and itching of the female genital area. In rare cases, lower abdominal pain can occur. Symptoms usually appear in women within five to twenty-eight days of exposure. A pelvic exam can reveal small red sores on the vaginal wall or cervix. Trichomoniasis can usually be cured with the prescription drug metronidazole.

# About the Authors

**Alexa Joy Sherman** has written for millions of women of all ages as senior editor of (and now, frequent contributor to) America's number-one women's fitness magazine, *Shape*, and—previously—as senior editor of the teen magazine "for girls who dare to be real," *Jump*. Prior to that, she spent six years in the music industry, working for Capitol Records and as senior editor of the trade magazine *HITS*. She has interviewed such luminaries as k.d. lang, Chris Isaak, and No Doubt, and written articles on everything from being a late bloomer to adventure cruising in Alaska to getting a better butt. Her work has appeared in all of the aforementioned publications, as well as in *Marie Claire* and *O, The Oprah Magazine*. Alexa shares a home with her husband, Joel, and their dog, Sydney, in Los Angeles.

**Nicole Tocantins** worked as a production coordinator at *HITS* (where she and Sherman met) for fourteen years. She now runs her own music supervision company for film and television and is also a stellar comedic actress. She has served as a music consultant for *Ally McBeal* and for motion pictures *All Over the Guy*, *Jackass*, and *Happy Endings*. Her feature film work includes roles in *The Opposite of Sex*, *Bounce*, and *Happy Endings*, while her television credits include *Seinfeld*, *Dharma and Greg*, and *Time of Your Life*. She is an active member of the Los Angeles theater community, where she costarred in the relationship comedy *I Know You Are, But What Am I?*, among other productions. Nicole lives in Los Angeles with her boyfriend and her dog, Ruby.

# *Index*

One-night stands, definition of, 4.
  *See also* Casual sex
Online dating, 120-22
Oral sex
  condoms and dental dams for, 44-45
  suggestions for, 208-10
  vomiting during, 219, 221
Orgies, 106-7

## P

Pap tests, 37
Parties
  Happy Hook-Up, 252-53
  meeting men at, 115-16
Pediculosis pubis. *See* Lice
Pelvic inflammatory disease (PID),
      285-86
Penetration princesses, 208
Penises
  size of, 144-45, 148, 208
  soft, 220-21
Periods, 216
Phone numbers, exchanging, 239-44,
      268, 278
Pickup lines
  to avoid, 140, 171-72
  to try, 168-71
PID (pelvic inflammatory disease),
      285-86
Pill, the, 45, 47
Playas, 22
Pope-sex, 211
Pornography
  foreign, 120
  losers and, 146, 150-51
Power, asserting your, 30, 136
Pregnancy, preventing, 45, 47
Pubic hair, 50

Public
  breakfast in, 238-39
  sex in, 193-98, 200

## Q

Queef, 68
Quiz, 11-16

## R

Radakovich, Anka, 44, 45, 99, 187
Regrets, 248, 253, 279
Rejection
  decreasing chances of, 165-73
  handling, 162-64
  hotline number, 243-44
  possibility of, 159-62
Relationships, 263-64, 268, 277.
      *See also* Exes
Restrooms, 193, 194, 197-98, 199
Richards, Mary, 6
Rimming, 218

## S

S.A.T. (Sexual Aptitude Test), 11-16
Scabies, 286
Scents, arousing, 165-67
Scoring, 4
Self-confidence, 172-73
Service providers, 96
Sex. *See also* Casual sex; Sexual
      encounters
  acts to avoid, 150-52
  dangers of, 34
  locations for, 175-201
  love vs., 27, 28-29
Sex and the City, 7, 13, 195-98
Sexile, 178